American Sign Language

A Student Text
Units 1-9

Dennis Cokely
Charlotte Baker-Shenk

Clerc Books
Gallaudet University Press
Washington, D.C.

Clerc Books
An imprint of Gallaudet University Press
Washington, DC 20002

Originally published 1980 by T. J. Publishers, Inc., Silver Spring Maryland
Published 1991 by Gallaudet University Press.
Printed in the United States of America

07 05 03 01   7 6 5 4

Cover design by Auras Design, Washington, D.C.
Drawings by Frank A. Paul
Photographs by Thomas Klagholz

Photograph of Charlotte Baker-Shenk taken by Viki Kemper.

ISBN 0-930323-86-6

CONTENTS

PREFACE

This text is part of a total, multi-media package designed for the teacher and student of American Sign Language (ASL). Included in this package are two texts for teachers and three texts for students:

American Sign Language: a teacher's resource text on grammar and culture

American Sign Language: a teacher's resource text on curriculum, methods, and evaluation

American Sign Language: a student text (Units 1-9)

American Sign Language: a student text (Units 10-18)

American Sign Language: a student text (Units 19-27)

Also included in this package is a set of five one-hour videotapes which are especially designed to accompany these texts.

As a package, the texts and videotapes provide the teacher with information about the structure of ASL and an interactive approach to teaching the language. They provide the student with carefully prepared ASL dialogues and drills as well as information about the structure of ASL and the Deaf Community.

The videotapes are designed so that there is a one-hour tape for each text. The first tape illustrates all of the examples in the grammar and culture text. The second tape provides a 'live' demonstration of a number of the techniques described in the curriculum, methods, and evaluation text. Each of the final three tapes (one for each student text) not only illustrates the dialogues for a particular text but also provides several ASL stories, poems, and dramatic prose of varying length and difficulty for use in the classroom or language lab.

ACKNOWLEDGEMENTS

It is simply not possible to mention all those individuals whose support and encouragement have made this text possible. Likewise, it would be very difficult to list all those individuals whose own ideas and creativity have influenced this text. However, there are several people we wish to mention by name because of their invaluable assistance in preparing this text:

For their creativity, spontaneity, and hard work in making the videotapes upon which this text is based—Larry Berke, Nathie Couthen, Pat Graybill, Ella Lentz, M. J. Bienvenu, and Gil Eastman.

For their patience during long photo sessions and their skill as models of ASL—two native, Deaf Signers: M. J. Bienvenu and Mel Carter, Jr.

For his unique artistic skills, beautiful illustrations, and willingness to keep doing more than what was expected—Frank Allen Paul.

For support, encouragement, and willingness to "pitch in"—Micky Cokely.

For his "good eye" and many hours spent in producing all of the beautifully clear photographs in this text—Tom Klagholz

For typing parts of the final draft—Sharon Church, Barbara LeMaster, and Mary Powell.

Finally, for typing, re-typing, and more re-typing of various drafts as well as for back rubs, amaranth seeds, and unfailing good cheer during the past two years—Beverly Klayman.

Note To the Teacher:

This text is intended to help your students acquire a certain level of skill in some of the major grammatical features of ASL. Each of the nine units focuses on a different grammatical topic in the language. Since this text is part of a three text series, not all aspects of a particular grammatical feature are covered in this text. Rather, these texts form the core of a spiraling curriculum. Thus, the same grammatical topics are covered in each of the three student texts. However, the discussion of each topic becomes more and more complex and detailed as the student progresses on to each higher-level text. There are a total of twenty-seven units (nine units per text) in this series. Each unit focuses on different aspects of the grammar of ASL and the culture of Deaf people.

The format of each unit is described in the section entitled *Note To the Student*. As mentioned in that section, we believe this format allows for a great deal of flexibility. Since you know your own teaching style and how your students learn best, we urge you to use this text in the way you feel is most beneficial. We do recommend that you go through this text at a slower pace than you may be accustomed to. As you look through the text, you will see that there is a lot of information in each unit. Please don't feel that you must go through one unit in each class or each week. We also suggest that you supplement the dialogues and drills with other activities that will reinforce the specific grammatical feature of each unit.

Our aim and hope is that the information provided in each unit will, for the most part, be dealt with by the students on their own time. This will free you to devote more class time toward developing their skills in *using* ASL instead of *talking about* ASL.

The two teacher texts (*Grammar and Culture* and *Curriculum, Methods, and Evaluation*) are an invaluable resource for using these student texts. The *Grammar and Culture* text not only provides a more detailed explanation of each of the grammatical features in the student texts, but it also contains several chapters of vital information that is not covered in these texts. In addition, at the end of each of the grammatical chapters, it contains a more complete transcription of each of the three student-text dialogues which focus on that grammatical topic. The *Curriculum, Methods and Evaluation* text not only explains how to conduct dialogues and drills in the classroom, but also shows you how to develop your own dialogues and drills. In addition, that text contains a large number of activities and exercises which can be used to supplement the dialogues and drills in the student texts.

As you skim through this text one thing should be quite obvious—this is not a vocabulary text. Although there are a large number of *Key Illustrations* and *Supplementary Illustrations,* these do not illustrate every sign that is used in the dialogues. Instead, it is assumed that either your students already know the vocabulary that is not illustrated or that you will provide them with this vocabulary by whatever means you feel is appropriate (use of a reference text, instruction in the classroom, etc.).

One final note: As you may know, variation in a language is the rule rather than the exception. There are always interesting differences in the vocabulary and grammar of different speakers or signers of a language. With this in mind, we have tried to include variations in signs wherever possible so that students will be able to understand a wider variety of ASL Signers. However, due to the limitations of space (and our knowledge), the treatment of sign variation in this text will need your reinforcement and expansion. We ask that you supplement the illustrations found in this text with other variations that you are aware of—especially those used by members of the Deaf Community in your area of the country.

Note To the Student:

Learning a second language is not an easy task. In fact, although learning your first language was probably the easiest thing you've ever done, learning a second language may be among the most difficult things you ever do. Learning a second language (and learning it really well) means learning more than the vocabulary and the grammar of that language. It means learning about the people who use that language—their attitudes, their cultural values, and their way of looking at the world.

Thus, learning American Sign Language as a second language means learning about the group of people who use ASL—the Deaf Community. It means recognizing the Deaf Community as a separate, cultural group with its own set of values, attitudes, and world view. Whatever your personal or professional motivations for wanting to learn ASL, you will find that the more you know about, appreciate, and understand the people who use ASL, the easier it is for you to learn their language.

For most hearing people, learning ASL is quite a different experience than learning a spoken language. First of all, to understand someone who is using ASL, you have to "listen" with your eyes. Most hearing people don't have a lot of experience at this since they have grown up depending mostly on their ears to receive linguistic information. Second, to produce ASL you have to use your eyes, face, hands, and body in ways which are not required by spoken languages. Most hearing people tend to be somewhat inhibited about using their eyes, face, hands, and body for communication. This is especially true for many Americans who have learned that "it is impolite to stare" and who have learned to restrain their body movements in order to be more socially acceptable.

Another important difference is that ASL is not a written language. This means that there are no newspapers, magazines, books, etc., written in ASL. Because ASL does not have a written form, we generally have to use English to write about ASL. This means using English words (called "glosses") when trying to translate the meaning of ASL signs and for trying to write down ASL sentences.

Although this is unavoidable at the present time, it has often led people to the mistaken notions that ASL is "bad English" or "broken English" because the grammar doesn't look like English—yet the "words" (signs) are written with English glosses. A real problem! Unfortunately, using English glosses for ASL signs also often leads students to think that ASL is very much like English, when, in fact, it is very different in many important ways.

Remember, the key to successfully learning any second language is: *accept the language on its own terms with an open mind*. If you have an open mind and an accepting attitude, and if you give yourself time, you will learn ASL. Of course, if you are trying to learn ASL (or any language), the most helpful thing is to communicate as frequently as possible with people who use ASL. While no book can substitute for real, live, human interaction, this text provides you with what we feel is a valuable supplement—carefully developed dialogues which are examples of how Deaf people actually communicate using ASL.

This text (part of a series of three student texts), contains nine units. Each of these units focuses on a topic relating to the grammar of ASL and on some cultural aspect of the Deaf Community. The format for each of these units is as follows:

A. *Synopsis:*   A detailed summary of the dialogue in that Unit.

B. *Cultural Information:*   An explanation of the cultural topic which the dialogue focuses on.

C. *Dialogue:*   A presentation of the dialogue with the two Signers' parts on separate pages.

D. *Key Illustrations:*   Drawings of signs which have been specially prepared for the dialogue so that the face, hands, and body are exactly as they appear in the dialogue. (We have tried to use the best possible angle in all illustrations for presenting both the manual and non-manual aspects of each sign.)

E. *Supplementary Illustration:*   Additional drawings of signs that appear in the dialogue. However, the face or body may be slightly different than the way the signs are used in the dialogue.

F. *General Discussion:*   An explanation of the specific grammatical features of ASL which the dialogue focuses on.

G. *Text Analysis:*   A line-by-line analysis and discussion of the dialogue.

H. *Sample Drills:*   Three drills which provide an opportunity to practice the specific grammatical features described in that Unit.

I. *Video Notes:*   A discussion of some of the important things that are shown in the videotaped version of the dialogue (taken from the videotape designed to accompany this text).

We believe that this format allows you, the student, a great deal of flexibility in using this text. You probably know how you learn best and what you need to help you learn. If you find that this sequence does not best suit your needs, then we encourage you and your teacher to take the sections in the order you find most helpful. For example, you may choose to read the *Dialogue* first and then the *Synopsis* and *Text Analysis*. The point is that you should be actively involved in deciding how to work with the text—and not be controlled by it. Use it in whatever way will best help you learn ASL.

Finally, as you learn ASL, remember that it is the language of a unique cultural group of people. Whenever appropriate, try to improve your skills by interacting with members of that cultural group. Don't be afraid of making mistakes, but learn from your mistakes. And don't overlook your successes; learn from them too. We hope this text will help you not only develop skills in ASL, but also develop an appreciation and respect for the Deaf Community.

Transcription Symbols

In order to understand the dialogues and drills in this text, you will need to read through the following pages very carefully. These pages describe and illustrate the transcription symbols that are used in this text.

You can imagine how difficult it is to "write ASL". To date, there is no standard way of writing ASL sentences. We have tried to develop a transcription system which clearly shows how much information is given in an ASL sentence. Although we have tried to keep this transcription system as simple as possible, it may still seem complex at first. However, with patience and practice, it will become fairly easy to use.

The chart on the following pages lists twenty-seven symbols, with examples and illustrations of how each symbol is used. To read this chart, you should first look at the illustrations of signs and the symbols used to describe them on the left-hand page, and then read through the explanation of each symbol on the right-hand page. The symbols found on these pages describe what the *hands* are doing. (In the parenthesis following the description, we have indicated the first unit in which each symbol appears.) Throughout the text in the *General Discussion* sections, symbols will be introduced which describe what the *eyes, face, head,* and *body* do.

ILLUSTRATIONS

KNOW

FROM-NOW-ON

NOT HERE

#WHAT

DIFFERENT+++

BORED*

TRANSCRIPTION SYMBOLS

Symbol	Example	Explanation
CAPITAL LETTERS	**KNOW**	An English word in capital letters represents an ASL sign; this word is called a *gloss*. (Unit 1)
-	**FROM-NOW-ON**	When more than one English word is needed to gloss an ASL sign, the English words are separated by a hyphen. (Unit 1)
△	△	A triangle with a letter inside is used to indicate a name sign. (Unit 1)
-	**P-A-T**	When an English word is fingerspelled, the letters in the word are separated by a hyphen. (Unit 2)
⌣	**NOT͜HERE**	When two glosses are joined by these curved lines, it indicates that two signs are used in combination. Generally when this happens, there is a change in one or both of the signs so that the combination looks like a single sign. (Unit 1)
#	**#WHAT**	When this symbol is written before a gloss, it indicates the sign is a fingerspelled loan sign. (Unit 1)
+	**DIFFERENT+++**	When a plus sign follows a gloss, this indicates that the sign is repeated. The number of plus signs following the gloss indicates the number of repetitions— e.g. **DIFFERENT+++** indicates the sign is made four times (three repetitions). (Unit 1)
*	**BORED***	An asterisk after a gloss indicates the sign is stressed (emphasized). (Unit 2)

"WHAT"

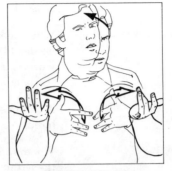

(2h) WHAT'S-UP

(2h)alt.GUESS

rt-**ASK-TO**-*lf*

ASSEMBLE-TO-*cntr*

Symbol	Example	Explanation
,	**YESTERDAY, ME**	A comma indicates a grammatical break, signaled by a body shift and/or a change in facial expression (and usually a pause). (Unit 1)
" "	**"WHAT"**	Double quotes around a gloss indicate a gesture. (Unit 1)
(2h)	(2h)**WHAT'S-UP**	This symbol for 'two hands' is written before a gloss and means the sign is made with both hands. (Unit 1)
alt.	(2h)alt.**GUESS**	The symbol 'alt.' means that the hands move in an 'alternating' manner. (Unit 5)

Symbol	Example	Explanation
rt *lf* *cntr*	*rt*-**ASK-TO**-*lf* **ASSEMBLE-TO**-*cntr*	The symbol *'rt'* stands for 'right'; *'lf'* for 'left'; and *'cntr'* for 'center'. When a sign is made *in* or *toward* a particular location in space, that place or direction is indicated after the gloss. When a symbol like *'rt'* is written before a gloss, it indicates the location where the sign began. So *rt*-**ASK-TO**-*lf* indicates that the sign moves from right to left. These symbols refer to the Signer's perspective—e.g. *'rt'* means to the Signer's right. The symbol *'cntr'* is only used when that space directly between the Signer and Addressee represents a particular referent (person, place, or thing). If none of these symbols appear, the sign is produced in neutral space. (Unit 1)

pat-ASK-TO-lee

me-CAMERA-RECORD-arc

me-SHOW-arc-lf

3-CL

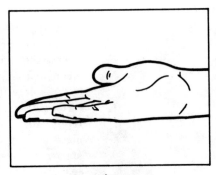

B↑-CL

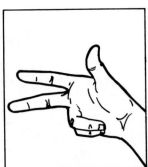

3→CL

Symbol	Example	Explanation
lower case words	*pat*-**ASK-TO**-*lee*	Italicized words that are connected (via hyphens) to the gloss for a verb can also indicate the location where the verb began or ended. For example, if 'Pat' has been given a spatial location on the right, and 'Lee' is on the left, then the sign *pat*-**ASK-TO**-*lee* will move from right to left. These specific words are not used until the things they represent have been given a spatial location. These specific words are used in place of directions like *'rt'* or *'lf'*. (Unit 1)
arc	*me*-**CAMERA-RECORD**-*arc* *me*-**SHOW**-*arc-lf*	When a gloss is followed by the symbol *'arc'*, it means the sign moves in a horizontal arc from one side of the signing space to the other side. If another symbol like *lf* follows the symbol *arc*, it means the arc only includes that part of the signing space. (Unit 3)
-CL	**3-CL**	This symbol for *classifier* is written after the symbol for the handshape that is used in that classifier. (Unit 5)
↑	**B↑-CL**	An arrow pointing upward indicates that the palm is facing upward. (Unit 6)
→	**3→CL**	An arrow pointing to the right indicates that the fingers are not facing upwards. This is used to distinguish two sets of classifiers: **3-CL** and **3→CL**; **1-CL** and **1→CL**. (Unit 5)

**1-CL'person come up
to me from rt'**

5:↓-CL@*rt*

5:↓-CL ⟶
B-CL↔'*street*'

Symbol	Example	Explanation
' '	**1-CL**'person come up to me'	Single quotes around a lower case word or words is used to help describe the meaning of a classifier in the context of that sentence. (Unit 5)
@	**5:↓-CL**@*rt*	This symbol indicates a particular type of movement that is often used when giving something a spatial location. It is characterized by a certain tenseness and a 'hold' at the end of the movement. In this example, the classifier for a large mass is given a spatial location to the Signer's right. (Unit 5)
CAPITAL LETTERS	**RESTAURANT** *INDEX-lf*	When a sign is made with the non-dominant hand, it is written in italics. When an italicized gloss is written under another gloss, it means both hands make separate signs at the same time. In this example, the dominant hand makes the sign **RESTAURANT** while the non-dominant hand points to the left. (Unit 1)
⟶	**5:↓-CL**⟶ *B-CL*↔*'street'*	An arrow proceeding from a gloss means that the handshape of that sign is held in its location during the time period shown by the arrow. In this example, the dominant hand 'holds' the **5:↓** classifier in its location while the non-dominant hand indicates a 'street' with the '**B**' handshape classifier. The symbol ↔ means that the '**B**' handshape moves back and forth. (Unit 3)

WAIT *"long time"*   **DISCUSS-WITH**
                              "each other" +"regularly"

$$\frac{q}{\textbf{RIGHT}}$$

Symbol	Example	Explanation
" "	"open window"	Double quotes around a word or words in lower case indicate a mimed action. (Unit 9)
" "	**WAIT**"*long time*"	Double quotes around an italicized word or words in lower case after a gloss indicates that a specific movement is added to that sign. The word or words inside the parentheses is the name for that specific movement. (Unit 8)
" "+" "	**DISCUSS-WITH** "*each other*"+"*regularly*"	When a plus sign joins two or more specific movements, it means those movements occur simultaneously with that sign. (Unit 8)
————	$\overline{\text{RIGHT}}^{\text{q}}$	A line on top of a gloss or glosses means that a certain non-manual (eyes, face, head, body) signal occurs during the time period shown by the line. At the end of the line, there is a letter(s) which indicates what the non-manual signal is. For example, '*q*' represents the signal for a particular type of question. (Unit 1)
( )	(gaze lf) △-*lf*	Words in parentheses on top of a gloss or glosses are used to indicate other movements of the eyes, head, and body. (The word 'gaze' refers to where the Signer looks.) (Unit 1)

INTRODUCTION TO AMERICAN SIGN LANGUAGE AND THE DEAF COMMUNITY

American Sign Language (also called ASL or Ameslan) is a *visual-gestural* language created by Deaf people and used by approximately 250,000–500,000 Americans (and some Canadians) of all ages. Some questions that students often ask are: Where did ASL come from? Who started it? Do all deaf people use ASL? To answer these questions, let's examine what is known about the history of ASL and the community of people who use this language.

A. History of American Sign Language

George W. Veditz, a Deaf teacher who became the President of the National Association of the Deaf in 1904, said, "As long as we have Deaf people, we will have Sign Language". Research on signed languages in many different countries shows us that Veditz was right. Throughout history, wherever there have been Deaf people, there have been signed languages: Chinese Sign Language (CSL), French Sign Language (FSL), Danish Sign Language (DSL), and so on. In fact, some scientists believe that the first languages that humans used in pre-historic times were gestural languages.

Unfortunately, there is very little information available about the deaf people who lived in America prior to 1817. We do know that between 2,000 and 6,000 deaf people were living in this country in the early 1800's. Some of them probably came from Europe or the British Isles; undoubtedly, others were born here. Then, during these early years of the 1800's, things began to happen which later led to the formation of an American Deaf Community. These events began with the meeting of Thomas Gallaudet and Alice Cogswell in Hartford, Connecticut.

Thomas H. Gallaudet, a graduate of Yale University, was studying to become a minister. His neighbor, Mason Cogswell, a well-known doctor in Hartford, had a deaf daughter named Alice. Gallaudet met Alice one day and tried to teach her to read and write a few words, and he had some success.

Dr. Cogswell was impressed with Gallaudet's work and encouraged him to consider starting a school for deaf children. Years earlier, the Clergymen's Association of Connecticut had reported that there were about 89 deaf people in the state. The need for a school was clear. So Cogswell and a group of concerned citizens raised enough money to send Gallaudet to Europe to learn about methods for instructing deaf people.

After several unsuccessful attempts to persuade the directors of the Braidwood schools in Great Britain to divulge their own methods of instructing deaf students (which focused on lip reading and speech training), Gallaudet went to Paris. He went to Paris because, while in London, he had seen an impressive demonstration of the French method of instructing deaf students. This method used signs from French Sign Language (the language of French Deaf people) with an added set of signs called *les signes méthodiques* ("methodical signs"). This set of "methodical signs" was invented by Abbé Charles de l'Epée, the founder and director of the first school for deaf students in Paris. Abbé de l'Epée created these "methodical signs" to represent certain grammatical words or parts of words that were used in spoken and written French but did not have sign equivalents in French Sign Language.

While in Paris, Gallaudet not only began to learn French signs but also studied the teaching methods used at the Paris school. After awhile, however, he wanted to return to Hartford; so he persuaded a Deaf man named Laurent Clerc, who was an instructor at the school, to go to Hartford with him to help establish a school for American deaf students. During the voyage to America, Laurent Clerc continued to teach signs to Gallaudet and Gallaudet taught Clerc English.

On April 15, 1817, with funds from the state of Connecticut, the U.S. Congress, and other sympathetic groups, Gallaudet and Clerc established the Institution for Deaf Mutes. This school was later renamed the American Asylum at Hartford for the Education and Instruction of the Deaf and Dumb and is presently called the American School for the Deaf. Clerc, who only intended to stay in America for a short time, remained there as an instructor for over forty years.

Until very recently, it was supposed that deaf people in America suddenly started learning and using French signs in 1817 and that they did not know or use any kind of signed language before Clerc and Gallaudet established the Hartford School. However, there is increasing evidence which shows that there must have been at least one signed language used in America before the Hartford School was established. Recent work done by a New England anthropologist shows that by 1817, deaf individuals on Martha's Vineyard had been actively participating in the social and political activities of that island for well over a century. According to the anthropologist, this active participation was possible because between the late 1600's and the early 1900's, the people on Martha's Vineyard lived in a bilingual community—a community where both spoken English and a signed language were commonly used.[1] The children in this community learned signs as they were growing up from both deaf and hearing adults in the surrounding area. Sign Language was used at town meetings, church services, informal gatherings at the post office and general store, etc. Often hearing people would sign to each other even when there were no deaf people around. This research indicates rather strongly that there was an active, flourishing Sign Language in America for well over a century before Clerc and Gallaudet introduced French signs.

In addition to this remarkable piece of evidence, there is also evidence that comes from looking at *cognates*—words or signs in one language that are historically

---

[1]Groce, N. 1980 "Everyone Here Spoke Sign Language" *Natural History* Vol. 89, No. 6, p. 10–16.

related to words or signs in another language. For example, the English words 'house', 'fish', and 'green' come from the German words 'Haus', 'Fisch', and 'grune'. By studying the number of cognates in two languages, it is possible to determine how much those two languages are related to each other. If American Sign Language (ASL) is directly descended from French Sign Language (FSL), then a high percentage of signs in ASL should be historically related to signs in FSL. A linguist at the Linguistics Research Laboratory at Gallaudet College decided to investigate the number of ASL-FSL cognates.[2] It was found that only about 60% of the signs in ASL seem to be related to signs in FSL. While it is true that languages change over time, natural language change during the last 160 years could not account for a difference of 40% —thus making it less likely that modern ASL was descended only from FSL.

A third piece of evidence comes from Clerc himself. There are accounts of Clerc lamenting the fact that his "graceful signs" were being changed and replaced, and that other signs which he did not teach were being used. Apparently, at least some deaf people already had a knowledge of signs before Clerc began teaching French signs. These deaf people probably combined their signs with French signs and that combination became Old American Sign Language.

Just as all 'living' languages change as people use them to communicate about the world (which also changes), Old ASL then evolved into what is now called Modern ASL. There are numerous examples of how older signs have changed as well as several examples of changes in the grammar of Old ASL. Thus, although Old ASL was heavily influenced by French signs, it is incorrect to say that ASL was "brought to America" by Clerc and Gallaudet. Rather, the French signs they brought were combined with the signs that deaf people in America were already using. This historical progression to Modern ASL is illustrated below:

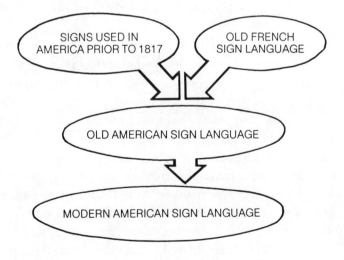

---

[2]Woodward, J. 1978 Historical bases of American Sign Language. In P. Siple (Ed.) *Understanding Language Through Sign Language Research*. New York: Academic Press, p. 333–348.

This is obviously a very condensed summary of the history of ASL. However, it does point out several important things about the language. First, ASL was not invented by someone and then given to deaf people in the U.S. Rather, it has evolved naturally from the signed languages of Deaf people in America and in France and was heavily influenced by French signs (just as English has been influenced by Latin, German, etc.). Second, Deaf people who use ASL have certain feelings or intuitions about what is acceptable in their language (since, for example, they did not wholeheartedly accept all of the signs that Clerc used). Just as no speaker of English would accept a word like 'tqsble', there are restrictions on what will be accepted into ASL. Third, Deaf people who use ASL will make changes in the language if these changes do not go against their feelings or intuitions about what is acceptable in ASL. Thus, Old ASL has changed during the past 160 or so years to become Modern ASL.

Every language has a special relationship with the group of people who use that language. The language reflects who those people are, what they value, and how they think about themselves and the world around them. Some scholars even refer to a language as the "soul" of the community of people who live with and use that language. Who are the people who use American Sign Language? The American Deaf Community.

B. What is the Deaf Community?

Defining the Deaf Community is a complex task. There does not seem to be a single distinguishing characteristic that all members of the community share. For example, the Deaf Community is not like an ethnic group where it is generally clear whether or not a person is a member—e.g., of the Black Community, the Jewish Community, etc. Instead, there seem to be a number of factors which must be considered when trying to understand who are the members of the Deaf Community.

One factor which does seem to be very important for understanding who is a member of the Deaf Community is called *attitudinal deafness*. This occurs when a person identifies him/herself as a member of the Community and when other members accept that person as part of the Community. Of course, to identify yourself with any group and to be accepted by that group means that you accept and support the values and goals of that group. Thus, someone who is a member of the Deaf Community accepts and supports the values and goals of the Community. This factor seems to be more important than whether or not a person is actually deaf. In fact, not everyone who is deaf is a member of the Deaf Community. Some individuals with a hearing loss prefer to identify with "the hearing world" and try to function as members of that group. Likewise, there are some hearing people who are considered part of the Deaf Community because they actively support the values and goals of the Deaf Community.

Among the basic values of the Deaf Community is its language—ASL. One very concrete way in which a person demonstrates acceptance and support for the values and goals of the Deaf Community is by showing respect for and acceptance of ASL. Obviously, one clear way to do this is to know and use ASL.

However, it has traditionally been very hard for an "outsider" (a hearing person) to learn ASL. Until recently, few classes really taught ASL. (Most classes taught a certain group of signs, but not the language that Deaf people really use.) And the only way to learn the language has been by interacting on a fairly continuous basis with members of the Deaf Community. But even that hasn't guaranteed success. Deaf people, in general, have been very cautious about using their language around hearing people and, thus, allowing them to learn it. The reason for this cautious attitude was clearly stated by a Deaf person (Barbara Kannapell) at the 1977 National Symposium on Sign Language Research and Teaching:

> It is important to understand that ASL is the only thing we have that belongs to Deaf people completely. It is the only thing that has grown out of the Deaf group. Maybe we are afraid to share our language with hearing people. Maybe our group identity will disappear once hearing people know ASL. Also, will hearing people dominate Deaf people more than before if they learn ASL?

It is not hard to understand this attitude when you realize that the Deaf Community has been dominated by hearing people in a number of ways—education, job opportunities, access to media, etc. The only area in which the Deaf Community has not been dominated is in the values and attitudes of the Community. Since the values and attitudes of the Community are shared through its language, ASL, it makes sense that Deaf people would be cautious about letting "outsiders" learn the language. If "outsiders" become fluent in the language, then they have a means of influencing the values and attitudes of the Community.

This should not discourage (hearing) people from wanting to learn ASL, but it should serve as a warning that some members of the Deaf Community may be initially reluctant or resistant to using ASL with them. This initial lack of enthusiasm on the part of some members of the Deaf Community may be considered a period of observation as they examine: What are the person's attitudes toward deafness? toward ASL? toward the Community? Of course, this observation often does not occur on a conscious level. But during this time, members of the Deaf Community form their own opinions about that individual and decide whether or not his/her attitudes, values, and goals are compatible with those of the Community. If they are, then the person is allowed to have closer and closer contact and interaction with the Community. If they are not, then contact and interaction is maintained on a more socially restricted or professional level.

In summary, then, the Deaf Community is a separate cultural group with its own values and set of shared experiences. Members of the Community are "attitudinally deaf"—which means they accept and support the values and goals of the Community. One concrete way in which a person demonstrates acceptance and support for the values and goals of the Community is by showing an acceptance and respect for the unique language of the Community—American Sign Language.

Unit 1

Sentence Types

A. Synopsis

Pat and Lee are co-workers in an office. They are on their coffee break. Pat asks Lee if Lee knows that a friend of theirs, △ , is moving away next week. Lee asks why △ is moving. Pat explains that △ has accepted a job in California at the residential school for Deaf students and will be switching jobs. Lee thinks that's great but asks Pat about the job. Pat replies that the superintendent of the school has quit and that △ will replace him. Lee asks whether their friend is going to sell his/her house, car, etc. Pat says that △ has already sold them. Lee then asks whether their friend has purchased a house in California yet. Pat says △ hasn't yet and explains that △ 's parents have a house in California and that △ will stay there for a couple of months. Lee agrees that △ should do that.

B. Cultural Information: Educational Programs for Deaf Students

The first school for Deaf students in the U.S. was started by a Deaf Frenchman (Laurent Clerc) and a hearing minister (Thomas Gallaudet). The school was founded in Hartford, Connecticut in 1817. Since that time, the number of schools and classes for Deaf students has increased tremendously. Today, almost every state has a residential school for Deaf students. Some of these schools are located on the same campus as the state residential school for Blind students. Generally, students live at the residential school during the week and return home on weekends. While at the school, they attend classes during the daytime and then are supervised by dorm counselors or houseparents during the late afternoon and evening. (See Unit 8 for further information.)

For many students, the residential school is the first exposure to the Deaf Community: it is where they make life-long friends (often including the person they will marry); it is often the place where they first experience sustained contact with Deaf adults; and it is where they learn and refine their ASL skills. Because of this, the residential school plays a very important role in sustaining the Deaf Community.

According to a 1980 survey[1], there are approximately 62 public and 6 private residential schools in the United States. These schools serve approximately 17,000 students from pre-school through high school. Until recently, the majority of Deaf students attended residential schools. Now, according to the 1980 survey, approxi-

---

[1]Craig, W. & H. Craig (Eds.) *American Annals of the Deaf*, Reference Issue, Vol. 125, No. 2, April 1980.

mately 7,500 students attend public or private day schools and 17,700 students attend public or private day classes.

The students in day schools or day classes are often "mainstreamed". (See Unit 7 for further information.) As a result, students now have less opportunities to become enculturated into the Deaf Community since they have fewer opportunities to interact with Deaf adults and Deaf peers. In fact, very few Deaf adults work in mainstreamed classes or schools. According to the 1980 survey, approximately 85% of all Deaf adults employed on the educational staffs of all educational programs work at residential schools, leaving only 15% in day programs.

However, the total number of Deaf adults in all educational programs is still very small. Educational programs for Deaf students in this country are, for the most part, dominated by hearing adults. The total number of educational personnel in programs cited in the 1980 survey is 13,362. The number of Deaf teachers is only 1,183 (11%). In addition, very few administrators or superintendents are Deaf.

C. Dialogue

Pat

Pat₁:

<u>   co   </u>   <u>   t </u>

"UMMM", **KNOW-THAT ONE-WEEK-FUTURE △ⱼ , MOVE-AWAY**-*rt*

Pat₂: **ACCEPT #JOB INDEX-*rt* CALIFORNIA STATE-SCHOOL, TRANSFER-TO-*rt***

Pat₃:

              <u>   (nodding)t </u>   (gaze lf)

SUPERINTENDENT INDEX-*rt*, QUIT-FROM-*rt*, △ⱼ-*lf* *j*-REPLACE-*superintendent*

Pat₄: **FINISH SELL FINISH**

Pat₅:

        <u> neg </u>   <u>   t </u>

(2h) NOT-YET, POSS-*lf* MOTHER⌒FATHER, HOUSE INDEX-*rt*,

MAYBE ONE-MONTH TWO-MONTH, *j*-MOOCH-FROM-*parents*

Lee

Lee₁: $\overline{\text{MOVE-AWAY-}lf \quad \text{FOR-FOR}}^{\text{wh-q}}$

Lee₂: FINEwg, $\overline{\text{"WHAT"} \quad \text{\#JOB} \quad \text{"WHAT"}}^{\text{wh-q}}$

Lee₃: △ HOUSE #CAR VARIOUS-THINGS $\overline{\text{\#DO-DO,}}^{\text{wh-q}}$ $\overline{\text{SELL}}^{\text{q}}$

Lee₄: $\overline{\text{FINISH} \quad \text{BUY} \quad \text{HOUSE} \quad \text{INDEX-}lf \quad \text{CALIFORNIA}}^{\text{q}}$

Lee₅: SHOULD+ WHY NOT

D. Key Illustrations

Pat

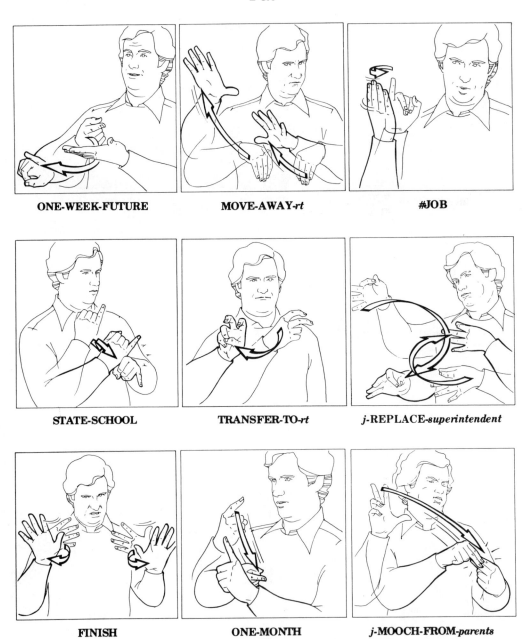

ONE-WEEK-FUTURE   MOVE-AWAY-*rt*   #JOB

STATE-SCHOOL   TRANSFER-TO-*rt*   *j*-REPLACE-*superintendent*

FINISH   ONE-MONTH   *j*-MOOCH-FROM-*parents*

Lee

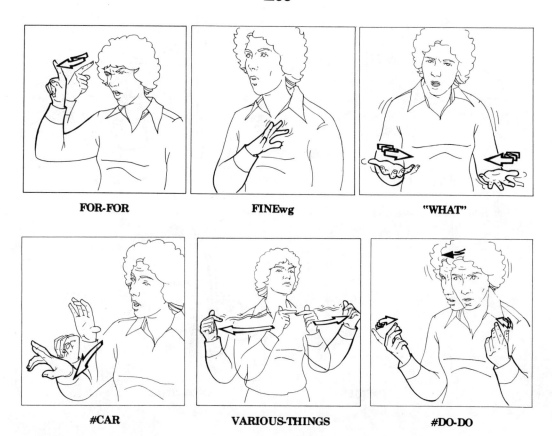

FOR-FOR   FINEwg   "WHAT"

#CAR   VARIOUS-THINGS   #DO-DO

E. Supplementary Illustrations

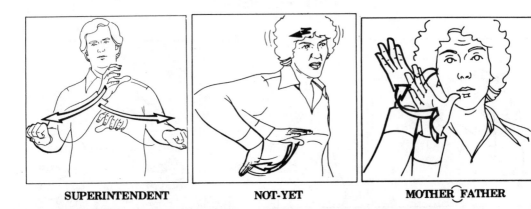

SUPERINTENDENT   NOT-YET   MOTHER FATHER

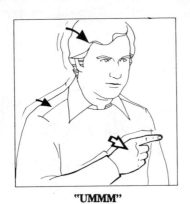
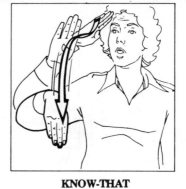

"UMMM"   KNOW-THAT

F. General Discussion: Sentence Types

ASL, like all languages, has grammatical signals to show whether a sentence is a question, or a command, or a negative statement, and so on. In ASL, these grammatical signals are both manual (using the hands) and non-manual (using the face and body.) Because it is not possible to describe all of these grammatical signals in one brief discussion, periodically throughout this text you will see explanations of some of the signals that are important for understanding each dialogue. At this point, however, we will begin to examine some of the major types of sentences and grammatical signals in ASL.

It is useful to think of the declarative statement as the most basic type of sentence in ASL. (An example of a declarative statement in English is 'Pat is happy'.) When a specific grammatical signal is added to a declarative statement, it changes the statement to another type of sentence—like a question, a negative, or a command. For example, 'yes-no' questions in ASL are made by adding the grammatical signal that we write as 'q'. The behaviors in this signal include a brow raise, 'widened eyes', and, frequently, a forward tilting of the head or body. The behaviors in this 'q' signal are illustrated in the following photographs.

$\overline{\text{YOU}}^{\text{q}}$ $\overline{\text{YOU}}^{\text{q}}$

Thus, a sentence like **FATHER ANGRY** ('Dad is angry') can become a question if the Signer adds these 'q' signal behaviors while signing the sentence.

q
_____
FATHER ANGRY   ('Is Dad angry?')

This type of question is called a 'yes-no' question because the answer can be either 'yes' or 'no'. Generally, the last sign in a question is also held longer than usual, and often that last sign is **YOU**—a reference to the person you are talking with. Occasionally a Signer will indicate that s/he is going to ask a question by using the opener *me-***ASK-TO**-*you,* which is illustrated below.

*me-***ASK-TO**-*you*

Another way to indicate that the sentence is a question is to use a manual question marker (**QM** or **QM**wg). The sign that we gloss as **QM** seems to be used in more formal situations while the other sign, **QM**wg, seems to occur more commonly. Often the sign **QM**wg is used to react to someone else's statement and can convey meanings like 'Really?!' or 'You gotta be kidding!'.

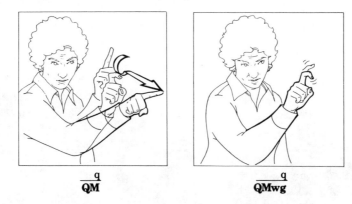

<table>
<tr><td>_____q
QM</td><td>_____q
QMwg</td></tr>
</table>

'Wh-word' questions (who, why, what, etc.) are made by adding the signal we write as '*wh-q*'. The behaviors in this signal include a brow squint and, frequently, a tilting of the head. The tilting of the head is often backwards or to one side. The behaviors in this '*wh-q*' signal are illustrated in the following photographs.

$$\overline{\text{WHERE}}^{\text{wh-q}} \qquad\qquad \overline{\text{WHICH}}^{\text{wh-q}}$$

In general, 'wh-word' signs occur at the end of the question. However, they sometimes occur at both the beginning and the end. Thus, a Signer may ask:

$$\overline{\text{ARRIVE WHEN}}^{\text{wh-q}} \qquad \text{or} \qquad \overline{\text{WHEN ARRIVE WHEN}}^{\text{wh-q}}$$

There is a general question sign in ASL that has a range of meanings: 'what', 'where', 'who', 'why', etc. This sign is written in quotes (**"WHAT"**) since it is actually a gesture which is often used by both hearing and Deaf people. There are, of course, specific signs like **WHY, WHEN, WHERE,** and **WHO,** and these will be described as they occur throughout the text.

$$\overline{\text{"WHAT"}}^{\text{wh-q}}$$

Commands in ASL are usually indicated by stressing or emphasizing the verb in the sentence and by maintaining direct eye contact with the person to whom the command is directed. (When a sign is stressed, we write an asterisk (*) after the gloss for that sign.) Sometimes, when the Signer wants to be *very* emphatic and firm, s/he will use a slower and very deliberate movement while looking sharply at the person.

Head nodding is often used to show agreement or to answer affirmatively ('yes') to a question. It is also used when the Signer is asserting that something is true. We write this non-manual behavior as *'nod'* for a single nod or *'nodding'* for repeated head nods. As you will see in the dialogues, nodding (or the negative behaviors described below) is frequently used to answer questions—sometimes while the Signer is still asking the question or just before signing a more complete response to the question.

Negative sentences are made by adding the signal we write as *'neg'*. The behaviors in this signal include a side-to-side headshake, and frequently, a frown, brow squint, 'wrinkled nose', and/or raised upper lip. The behaviors in the *'neg'* signal are illustrated in the following photographs.

neg
FEEL   neg
                  ME

This negative signal can be used without a manual, negating sign like **NOT** or **DON'T**. For example, the sentence **HUNGRY ME** can be negated by simply adding this negative signal.

neg
HUNGRY ME   ('I'm not hungry.')

However, there are also many negative signs. Three of these are illustrated below. The sign which is glossed as **DON'T** tends to be used in more formal contexts or in commands. The sign **NOT-YET** conveys the idea of 'not now, but maybe later'. Other negative signs will be discussed throughout the text.

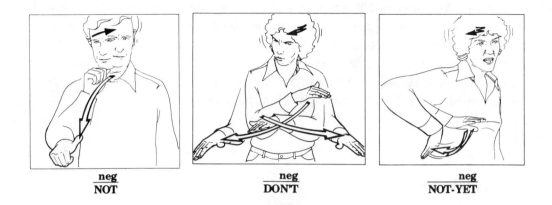

<table>
<tr><td align="center">neg
NOT</td><td align="center">neg
DON'T</td><td align="center">neg
NOT-YET</td></tr>
</table>

In general, ASL Signers tend to sign first the thing they want to talk about (this is called the "topic") and then make some statement or question, etc., about the topic. Signers can show what the topic is by using another non-manual grammatical signal ('t') while they sign the topic. During the signing of the topic, the brows are raised, the head is tilted, and the last sign of the topic is held slightly longer than normal—resulting in a pause. The non-manual behaviors in this signal are illustrated in the following photograph.

t
PAPER

After the topic has been signed, the head position and brows change. The sentence below illustrates this general pattern.

$$\overline{\quad\quad\quad\overset{t}{\quad\quad}\quad\overset{q}{\quad\quad}}$$
YOUR   HOUSE,   FAR   ('Is your house far away?')

The topic **YOUR HOUSE** occurs first with the non-manual behaviors in the topic signal, and then the Signer asks a question about the topic—('Is it far away?'). Examples of this topic signal will be seen throughout the dialogues in this text.

These are some of the basic grammatical signals in ASL which help to distinguish different types of sentences. As additional signals appear in the dialogues, they will be discussed in the *Text Analysis* notes that follow each dialogue.

G. Text Analysis

Pat$_1$: $\overline{\overset{co}{\quad\quad}}$ $\overline{\text{KNOW-THAT   ONE-WEEK-FUTURE}\ \triangle\ \overset{t}{,}\quad\text{MOVE-AWAY-}rt}$
           "UMMM",

• $\overline{\quad\quad\overset{co}{\quad\quad}}$
  "UMMM"

> This is an attention-getting conversational opener. It is similar to the gesture used by many people to express the meaning 'Oh, that's right, I wanted to tell you something'. The symbol *'co'* is used to indicate a sign or gesture which is used to get someone's attention and to begin a conversation.

• **KNOW-THAT**

> This sign comes from the two signs **KNOW** and **THAT**. The sign **KNOW-THAT** is frequently used to introduce the topic of a sentence.

• **ONE-WEEK-FUTURE**

> This sign moves along what has been called the "time line". Notice in the illustration that the sign moves forward 'into the future'. For further information about the time line, see Unit 2.

• $\triangle$

> This is an example of a name sign in ASL. Name signs are generally given to a person by members of the Deaf Community. Some name signs are based on a physical attribute of the person. There are also name signs which incorporate the initial letters of a person's first or last name. For example, the sign in this dialogue could be the name sign for someone called 'John' or 'Joan'. More information on name signs will be given throughout this text.

- $\overline{\text{KNOW-THAT}\quad\text{ONE-WEEK-FUTURE}\quad\overset{t}{\triangle}}$,

    Notice that this whole phrase is the topic of the sentence. That is, the Signer introduces this information in the beginning of the sentence and then will make some comment about it. Notice that the non-manual behaviors which indicate a topic occur during the whole phrase. These behaviors are described in the *General Discussion* section.

- **MOVE-AWAY-*rt***

    This is an example of a sign which can be moved to a specific location to show where something happens. For further discussion, see Unit 4. Notice that this sign 'comments on' or provides more information about the topic of the sentence.

Lee₁: $\overline{\text{MOVE-AWAY-}lf\quad\text{FOR-FOR}}^{\text{wh-q}}$

- **MOVE-AWAY-*lf***

    This is an example of how Signers generally will use the same locations in space to represent the same things. In this case, Pat made the sign to his/her right (the location where $\triangle$ is moving.) This location is to Lee's left. For further discussion, see Unit 3.

- **FOR-FOR**

    This sign is frequently used when the Signer wants to know what something is for, why someone is doing something, the reason for something, etc.

- $\overline{\text{MOVE-AWAY-}lf\quad\text{FOR-FOR}}^{\text{wh-q}}$

    Notice that this entire sentence is a 'wh-word' question. Consequently, the non-manual behaviors which are used with this type of question occur through the entire sentence. These non-manual behaviors are described in the *General Discussion* section above.

Pat₂: ACCEPT   #JOB   INDEX-*rt*   CALIFORNIA   STATE-SCHOOL,   TRANSFER-TO-*rt*

- **#JOB**

    This is an example of what is called a "fingerspelled loan sign" in ASL. Fingerspelled loan signs in ASL are 'borrowed' from fingerspelled English words and are changed so that they look more like ASL signs. Because of these changes, they are thought of as signs. The illustration of this particular loan sign shows that the middle letter ('O') has dropped out. This is quite common with fingerspelled loan signs. Other examples of loan signs will appear in other units.

- **TRANSFER-TO-*rt***

  This is an example of a verb in which the direction of movement indicates the subject and/or object. For more discussion of verbs of this type, see Unit 4.

$$\overline{\hspace{3cm}\text{wh-q}\hspace{3cm}}$$

Lee$_2$:   FINEwg,   **"WHAT"   #JOB   "WHAT"**

- **"WHAT"**

  This is the general interrogative (question) sign which was discussed above. The repetition of this sign before and after the thing being asked about is common in ASL.

$$\overline{\hspace{4cm}\text{wh-q}\hspace{2cm}}$$

- **"WHAT"   #JOB   "WHAT"**

  This is another example of a 'wh-word' question in ASL. Notice that the non-manual behaviors in the *wh-q* signal continue during the entire question.

$$\overline{\hspace{2cm}\text{(nodding)t}\hspace{2cm}}\qquad \overline{\hspace{0.5cm}\text{(gaze lf)}\hspace{0.5cm}}$$

Pat$_3$:   **SUPERINTENDENT   INDEX-*rt*,   QUIT-FROM-*rt*,   △-*lf*   j-REPLACE-*superintendent***

- **INDEX-*rt***

  In this example, the Signer points to ('indexes') the location of the state school in California to show that s/he is talking about the superintendent at that school. Pointing with the index finger also functions as a pronoun in ASL and is described more in Unit 3.

$$\overline{\hspace{6cm}\text{t}\hspace{0.5cm}}$$

- **SUPERINTENDENT   INDEX-*rt*,**

  Notice that the non-manual behaviors which occur with topics (brows raised, head tilted, and last sign held slightly longer) are used throughout this phrase.

- **QUIT-FROM-*rt***

  This is another example of a verb which can indicate what is the subject and/or object, much like the sign **TRANSFER-TO-*rt***. For more information, see Unit 4.

  (gaze lf)
- △-*lf*

  Notice that the Signer not only produces the name sign △ to the left but also gazes to the left. This use of eye gaze to 'assign' locations in space to people, places, and things is discussed further in Unit 3.

$$\text{Lee}_3: \quad \text{⚠} \quad \text{HOUSE} \quad \text{\#CAR} \quad \text{VARIOUS-THINGS} \quad \overline{\text{\#DO-DO,}}^{\text{wh-q}} \quad \overline{\text{SELL}}^{\text{q}}$$

- **#CAR**

  This is another example of a fingerspelled loan sign. Notice that the middle letter ('**A**') is barely recognizable, and that the other fingerspelled letters have been changed so that they run together more like a sign. As a result, the fingerspelled loan more closely resembles an ASL sign.

- $\overline{\text{\#DO-DO}}^{\text{wh-q}}$

  This is also a fingerspelled loan sign. In this context, it's most likely translation would be "What's s/he gonna do with 'em?". However, the sign can also convey the meanings 'What should I do?', 'What can we do?', 'What did s/he do?', etc. Notice that since this is a 'wh-word' question it is accompanied by the *wh-q* non-manual behaviors.

- $\overline{\text{SELL}}^{\text{q}}$

  This is an example of a 'yes-no' question in ASL and is made with the non-manual behaviors which were described above.

$$\text{Pat}_4: \quad \text{FINISH} \quad \text{SELL} \quad \text{FINISH}$$

- **FINISH**

  This sign, in its most common form, refers to the completion of an event and thus, indicates that something occurred in the past. This sign can also be made with a very tense movement or repeated tense movements and then has the meaning 'That's enough!' or 'Stop it!'.

$$\text{Lee}_4: \quad \overline{\text{FINISH} \quad \text{BUY} \quad \text{HOUSE} \quad \text{INDEX-}\textit{lf} \quad \text{CALIFORNIA}}^{\text{q}}$$

- **INDEX-***lf*

  This is another instance of pointing with the index finger. Notice that the Signer indexed (pointed to) the same location that was assigned earlier to California—to the left.

            neg   t

Pat₅: (2h) NOT-YET, POSS-*lf* MOTHER FATHER, HOUSE INDEX-*rt,*

MAYBE ONE-MONTH TWO-MONTH, *j*-MOOCH-FROM-*parents*

------
neg
- **NOT-YET**

  This sign is essentially the opposite of the sign **FINISH** and indicates that something is not completed but that the Signer plans to or is supposed to complete it. See Unit 2 for further discussion. Notice also that since this sign is a negative response to Lee's question, it is accompanied by the non-manual behaviors for negation.

- **MOTHER FATHER**

  This is an example of two separate signs acting together like one sign in a sentence. Usually when two signs are frequently used together, their forms change slightly. For example, the first part of the sign **MOTHER FATHER** is slightly different than the sign **MOTHER**. In addition, the meaning is usually different than the meaning of the two separate signs. For example, the meaning of this sign is not 'mother and father', but 'parents', which is slightly different. Over time, signs like this tend to become so changed that Signers do not recognize that they were originally created from two separate signs (e.g. **HOME** from **EAT** + **BED**).

- **TWO-MONTH**

  This is an example of number incorporation on a time sign. In ASL, it is possible to change the handshape of certain time signs to indicate specific periods of time. For further explanation, see Unit 2.

- *j*-**MOOCH-FROM**-*parents*

  This is another example of a sign which can indicate its subject and/or object by the direction of movement. In this case, △ has been previously located to Pat's left, and the parents' house in California has been assigned a location to Pat's right. The sign *j*-**MOOCH-FROM**-*rt* moves from Pat's left (the location of △) to Pat's right (the location of the parents and their house). So the movement of the verb shows that △ is the subject (△ does the 'mooching') and that the parents are the object (they are 'mooched from'). For further discussion of verbs like this, see Unit 4.

H. Sample Drills

<div markdown>

1. <u>   wh-q</u>
    MOVE-AWAY-*lf* **FOR-FOR**
    |
    <u>   wh-q</u>
    "WHAT"
    |
    <u>   wh-q</u>
    "DO-DO"
    |
    <u>wh-q</u>
    WHY
    |
    <u>   q</u>
    FINISH
    |
    <u>   neg</u>
    NOT-YET
    |
    <u>   wh-q</u>
    FOR-FOR

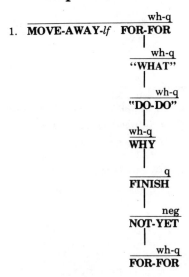

2.   **HOUSE**   **#CAR VARIOUS-THINGS** <u> wh-q </u> <u> q </u>
                                                          #DO-DO, SELL
    BICYCLE
                    BOOK
    CAR
                    BOAT
    CAT
                    #CAR
    HOUSE

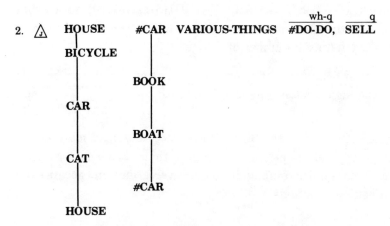

3. <u>   q</u>
    FINISH BUY HOUSE INDEX-*rt* **CALIFORNIA**
    |
    <u>   neg</u>
    NOT-YET,
    |
    <u>   wh-q</u>
    #DO-DO,
    |
    <u>   wh-q</u>
    FOR-FOR,
    |
    <u> q</u>
    MAYBE
    |
    <u>   t</u>
    ONE-WEEK-FUTURE,
    |
    <u> q</u>
    FINISH

I. Video Notes

If you have access to the videotape package designed to accompany these texts, you will notice the following:

- In Pat's first turn, the sign **ONE-WEEK-FUTURE** has another non-manual signal with it (in addition to the signal that shows it is part of the topic in the sentence). This signal (tilting the head forward toward the shoulder and raising the cheek and side of the mouth toward the shoulder) is used when the Signer wants to indicate that something is 'close in time' or 'close in space'.

- This name sign △ is produced on the wrist and in itself does not specify whether the person is male or female (like the name 'Pat' can be either male or female).

- In Pat's third turn, notice how the Signer gazes to the left to give △ a location to the left.

- In Lee's third turn (△ **HOUSE   #CAR   VARIOUS-THINGS**), notice that the Signer pauses slightly after each item in the list. This is quite common in ASL when Signers are listing a number of things.

- Notice the non-manual behaviors for expressing negation which can be seen quite clearly on the 'single shot' segment of Pat's fifth turn—_____ neg
(2h) **NOT-YET.**

In general, pay careful attention to the Signer's eye, face, and head movements. Notice also that the Signers tend to hold the last sign in their turn even while the other person is signing. This is quite common in ASL conversations and occurs even more frequently when asking questions.

Unit 2

Time

A. Synopsis

Pat and Lee are having dinner at a restaurant. Pat asks if Lee has read the *Deaf American* magazine. Lee replies that his/her subscription stopped last year and s/he hasn't paid to renew it. Pat says that Lee should renew the subscription because now the cover of the magazine is new—the artwork and the color. It's different than the old magazine. Lee asks to see it. But Pat left it at home. This morning Pat read it for half an hour and hasn't finished yet. Lee says that maybe next week s/he will join the National Association of the Deaf (NAD) and subscribe to the *Deaf American*. Pat states that after joining the NAD, Lee can go to the convention which is held every two years. Lee says that s/he has gone occasionally and will go to the convention two years from now. Pat asks why. Lee responds that at the convention two years from now, the NAD will have a centennial (100 year) celebration.

B. Cultural Information: The *Deaf American* and the National Association of the Deaf

The *Deaf American* is a magazine that is published monthly (except for a joint July-August issue) by the NAD. This national magazine contains items of interest to the Deaf Community such as: interviews with Deaf persons, sports results, general interest articles, legislation-related projects and activities, etc. This publication, along with newsletters published by state NAD chapters or local clubs, helps members of the Deaf Community keep up with what is happening in the Community on a national and local level.

The National Association of the Deaf (NAD) began in 1880 at the First National Convention of Deaf-Mutes in Cincinnati, Ohio. The first president of the NAD was Robert P. McGregor of Ohio. In 1952, the NAD opened its first home office in Chicago. In 1960, the Junior NAD was established to provide young Deaf people with training in citizenship and leadership. In September 1964, the home office of the NAD was re-located to Washington, D.C. The name of the NAD publication was changed from the *Silent Worker* to the *Deaf American*. In 1964, the NAD decided to hire its first full-time Executive-Secretary, Frederick C. Schreiber. In 1969, the NAD began publishing books and articles on deafness, the education of deaf people, manual communication, and other related topics. In 1971, the NAD moved into its present location, the Halex House in Silver Spring, Maryland. Currently, the NAD has about 17,000 members. For more information about the NAD and its activities, please write: National Association of the Deaf, 814 Thayer Avenue, Silver Spring, Maryland 20910.

C. Dialogue

Pat

Pat₁:
$$\overline{}^{\text{co}}^{\text{q}}$$

Pat₁:
    <u>co</u>   <u>q</u>
"HEY", FINISH READ-*paper* DEAF AMERICA YOU

Pat₂:
                                <u>t</u>   <u>t</u>
SHOULD, NOW DEAF AMERICA COVER, NEW+, COLOR, ART, DIFFERENT*

Pat₃:
<u>neg</u>
    LEAVE-IT-*rt* HOME INDEX-*rt*,

                                      <u>neg</u>
MORNING ME READ-*paper* HALF-HOUR, NOT-YET FINISH

Pat₄:
                <u>nodding+brow raise</u>   <u>nod</u> (gaze rt   )
PARTICIPATE-IN-*nad* FINISH, CAN GO-TO-*rt* MEETING EVERY-TWO-YEAR-FUTURE,

<u>nodding+q</u>
RIGHT

Pat₅:
                            <u>wh-q</u>
TWO-YEAR-FUTURE, WHYwg

Pat₆:
                <u>nod</u>
"THAT'S-RIGHT"

Lee

Lee₁: $\overline{\text{neg}}$ $\overline{\text{ONE-YEAR-PAST, ME   RECEIVE-REGULARLY,   STOP,   ME }}^{\text{t}}$ $\overline{me\text{-PAY-TO-}rt,}^{\text{t}}$

$\overline{\text{neg}}$
AGAIN

Lee₂: **SEE-SEE**

Lee₃: $\overline{\text{ONE-WEEK-FUTURE,   MAYBE   ME }}^{\text{t}}$ *me*-**PARTICIPATE-IN-***cntr* **N-A-D,**

$\overline{\text{ME   RECEIVE-REGULARLY   D-A}}^{\text{nodding}}$

Lee₄: $\overline{\text{ME   GO-TO-}lf}^{\text{nodding}}$ $\overline{\text{ONCE-IN-AWHILE,   "UMMM"   TWO-YEAR-FUTURE,}}^{\text{nodding}}$^{t}

ME   GO-TO-*lf*

Lee₅: $\overline{\text{THAT-ONE-}lf\text{   TWO-YEAR-FUTURE,}}^{\text{t}}$ **N-A-D   (2h)THRILL   ONE HUNDRED   YEAR   CELEBRATE**

D. Key Illustrations

Pat

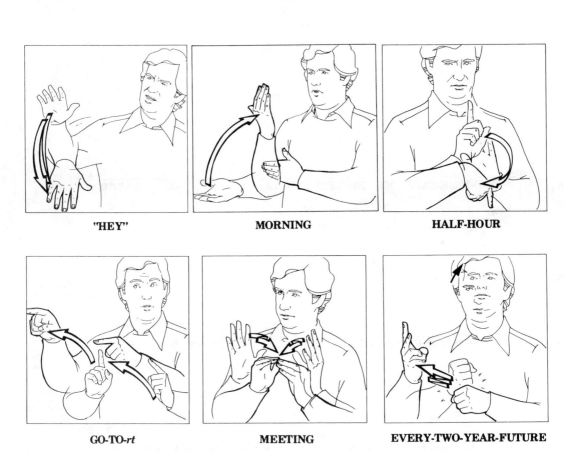

"HEY"   MORNING   HALF-HOUR

GO-TO-*rt*   MEETING   EVERY-TWO-YEAR-FUTURE

Lee

RECEIVE-REGULARLY

SEE-SEE

ONCE-IN-AWHILE

TWO-YEAR-FUTURE

(2h)THRILL

E. Supplementary Illustrations

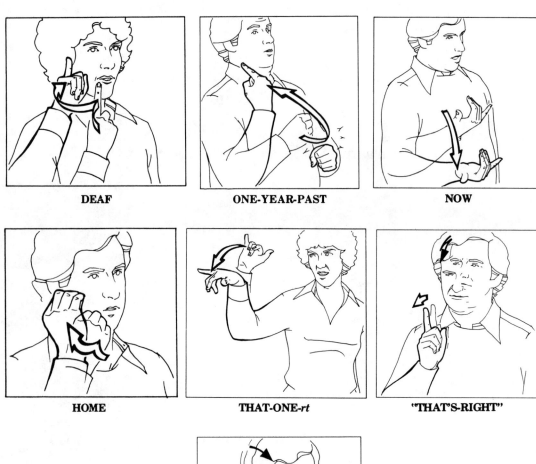

DEAF   ONE-YEAR-PAST   NOW

HOME   THAT-ONE-*rt*   "THAT'S-RIGHT"

"UMMM"

F. General Discussion: Time

Time signs in ASL are generally produced in relation to what has been called the *time line,* illustrated below.

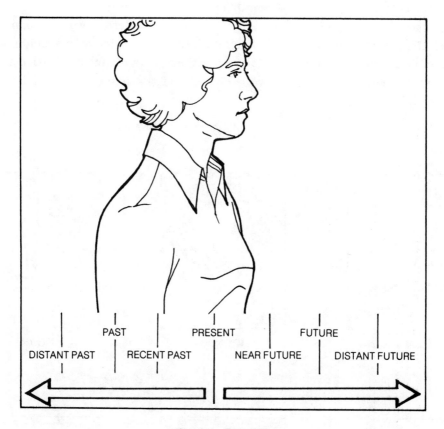

Fig. 2.1 Time Line

In general, the Signer's body represents present time. Signs that refer to present time (**NOW, TODAY**), to the recent past (**ONE-DAY-PAST, RECENTLY**), and to the near future (**ONE-DAY-FUTURE**) are made close to the body. Signs that refer to the distant future (**FUTURE, WILL**) are made further in front of the Signer's body. Signs that refer to the distant past (**PAST, LONG-TIME-AGO**) are made further toward the area behind the Signer's body. Thus, time signs or "time indicators" have a relative *location* on the time line which agrees with their meaning.

In addition to their location, the *direction of movement* of time signs also indicates their relation to present time. For example, the sign **ONE-DAY-FUTURE** moves forward (toward the 'future') while the sign **ONE-DAY-PAST** moves backward (toward the 'past'). (These signs are often glossed as **TOMORROW** and **YESTER-DAY**.)

For certain signs, the passive[1] or base hand becomes the point of reference and can represent a particular time (e.g. now, two weeks ago, next month). In such cases, the direction of movement of the active hand indicates time in relation to whatever time the passive hand represents. For example, the passive hand in the signs **BEFORE** or **AFTER** might represent the time 'last month'. Then the signs **BEFORE** or **AFTER** would mean 'before last month' or 'after last month'.

The passive hand and arm is used in a slightly different way in signs like **MORNING, NOON,** and **AFTERNOON**. With these signs, the active hand may be thought of as representing the relative positions of the 'sun' in relation to the 'horizon' (the passive hand and arm). This use of the passive hand and arm is illustrated below.

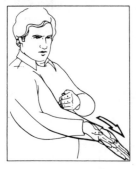
EARLY-MORNING

MORNING

NOON

AFTERNOON

EVENING

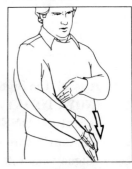
MIDNIGHT

---

[1]The *passive* hand is the hand that doesn't move—as opposed to the *active* hand which does move. The *dominant* hand of a right-handed Signer is the right hand; the *non-dominant* hand of a right-handed Signer is the left hand.

For some signs (those referring to 'clock time'), the flat palm of the passive hand can be thought of as the face of a clock. The index finger of the active hand marks off units of time on the 'clock face'. The signs **ONE-SECOND, ONE-MINUTE,** and **ONE-HOUR** are examples of this use of the passive hand.

ONE-SECOND

ONE-MINUTE

ONE-HOUR

In order to indicate a specific number of time units (**TWO-WEEK, THREE-HOUR, TWO-DAY,** etc.), handshapes for numbers are "incorporated" into the time sign. That is, the appropriate numeral handshape (2,3,4, etc.) is used as the handshape of the time sign.

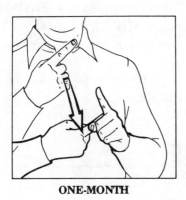

ONE-MONTH

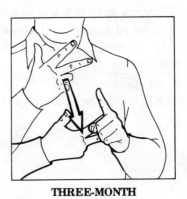

THREE-MONTH

The direction of movement of these number-incorporated time signs indicates whether the time unit is occurring in the past or in the future. For example, to express the meaning 'in two weeks' or 'two weeks into the future', the Signer would use the handshape for the number '2' in the sign that means 'week' and then move the sign forward (into the 'future').

| TWO-WEEK-PAST | TWO-WEEK-FUTURE (Variant A) | TWO-WEEK-FUTURE (Variant B) |

   Time signs that function as adverbs (telling when something happens) most frequently occur at the beginning (or close to the beginning) of the sentence in ASL. If a time is not specified in an ASL sentence, it is assumed that the verb is in the present tense. If a time is specified (e.g. with a sign like **ONE-DAY-PAST** or **TWO-WEEK-FUTURE**), then all of the events described by the Signer are understood as occurring at that time. This holds true not only for that sentence but for all subsequent sentences until a new time is specified. Thus, time signs are frequently used in ASL to establish the tense of a particular event or series of events.

   There are two general time signs in ASL which are used quite frequently and which indicate whether an action or event has already occurred (**FINISH**) or has not yet occurred (**NOT-YET**). These signs focus on the idea of 'completion'. The sign **FINISH** indicates that the action or event has been completed (e.g. **FINISH EAT ME**—'I finished eating' or 'I already ate'). The sign **NOT-YET** indicates a lack of completion, but (usually) an intention or need to complete that action or event (e.g.

$$\overline{\qquad\qquad\qquad\quad}^{\;t}\;\;\overline{\qquad\qquad}^{\;neg}$$
BOOK READ-book, **NOT-YET ME**—'I haven't yet read the book'). The nonmanual behaviors for negation usually occur with this sign.

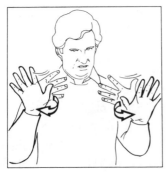

| FINISH | NOT-YET |

G. Text Analysis

Pat₁: <u> co </u>   <u>   q </u>

"HEY",   FINISH READ-*paper* DEAF AMERICA YOU

- <u>   co </u>
  "HEY"

  The gesture **"HEY"** (waving a hand to get someone's attention) is commonly used as a conversational opener in ASL. There are several other types of conversational openers, including tapping someone on the shoulder or lightly banging on a table.

- **FINISH**

  In this context, the Signer is asking whether the action (reading the magazine) is completed, or has already occurred. Notice that the non-manual behaviors for asking a 'yes-no' question occur throughout the entire question.

- **READ-*paper***

  This sign is glossed as **READ-*paper*** because of the similarity between this sign and signs such as **READ-*lips*, READ-*sign*,** etc. See Unit 4 for further discussion of signs of this type.

- **DEAF AMERICA**

  There are two basic forms of the sign **DEAF.** One is more formal, and the other is more informal. The sign used in this dialogue and illustrated above is the more informal one. Compare that sign with the more formal sign.

DEAF
(formal)

  An alternate way of referring to this magazine—the *Deaf American*—is to use the initials D.A. An example of this appears later in the dialogue.

- **YOU**

  As described in Unit 1, the sign **YOU** frequently occurs at the end of questions.

Lee₁:
$\overline{}^{\text{neg}}$ $\overline{\text{ONE-YEAR-PAST, ME RECEIVE-REGULARLY,}}^{\text{t}}$ STOP, ME $\overline{me\text{-PAY-TO-}rt,}^{\text{t}}$

$\overline{\text{AGAIN}}^{\text{neg}}$

- $\underline{\text{neg}}$

    Notice that the Signer responds to the question with the negative non-manual behaviors described in Unit 1. This is a good example of how some of these non-manual behaviors can be used without manual signs.

- $\overline{\textbf{ONE-YEAR-PAST ME RECEIVE-REGULARLY,}}^{\text{t}}$

    Notice that this entire phrase is accompanied by the non-manual behaviors used to indicate a topic (see Unit 1). The Signer then comments about or provides information pertaining to this topic.

    The sign **RECEIVE-REGULARLY** is used when discussing magazine subscriptions, receiving pension checks, social security checks, etc.

- $\overline{me\text{-}\textbf{PAY-TO-}rt}^{\text{t}}$

    This is an example of a verb which can indicate the subject and object by the direction of its movement. For example, by changing the direction of movement, one can sign *me*-**PAY-TO**-*you,* *you*-**PAY-TO**-*me,* etc. See Unit 4 for further discussion.

    Notice also that this sign occurs with the non-manual behaviors described in Unit 1 for indicating a topic. Thus, what follows is a comment or statement about this topic.

- $\overline{\textbf{AGAIN}}^{\text{neg}}$

    Notice that the sign **AGAIN** has been negated with the non-manual 'neg' signal.

Pat₃:
$\overline{}^{\text{neg}}$ LEAVE-IT-*rt* HOME INDEX-*rt,*

MORNING ME READ-*paper* HALF-HOUR, $\overline{\text{NOT-YET FINISH}}^{\text{neg}}$

- $\underline{\text{neg}}$

    Notice that Pat responds to Lee by using negative non-manual behaviors before starting to sign. See Unit 1 for a description of these behaviors.

- **LEAVE-IT**-*rt* **HOME INDEX**-*rt,*

    Notice that the directions of the sign **LEAVE-IT-**___and **INDEX-**___ are the same—to the right. That is, these two signs 'agree with each other' since they refer to the same place. If the sentence had been signed with **HOME INDEX**-*rt* first, then we would know that the location on the right represents 'home' and the sign **LEAVE-IT-**___ could have been glossed as **LEAVE-IT**-*home*. For further discussion of how some verbs in ASL use direction and location, see Unit 4.

• **MORNING**

Since no other time has been specified, the Signer is referring to something that happened *this* morning.

• **HALF-HOUR**

This is an example of the non-dominant hand functioning as a 'clock face' while the dominant hand indicates the specific time unit. Other examples of this use of the non-dominant hand are given in the *General Discussion* section above.

$$\overline{\hspace{3cm}\text{neg}}$$
• **NOT-YET   FINISH**

Used together in this context, the meaning of these two signs is that the action is not yet completed. Notice also that the non-manual behaviors for negation (Unit 1) occur with both signs. For further information on these two signs, see the *General Discussion* section above.

Lee$_3$: $\overline{\hspace{3.5cm}\text{t}}$
ONE-WEEK-FUTURE,   MAYBE   ME *me*-**PARTICIPATE-IN**-*cntr*   **N-A-D,**

$$\overline{\hspace{4.5cm}\text{nodding}}$$
ME   RECEIVE-REGULARLY   D-A

$$\overline{\hspace{3cm}\text{t}}$$
• **ONE-WEEK-FUTURE**

Notice how this time sign occurs at the beginning of the sentence and indicates when the action occurs (or is likely to occur). Notice also how this sign moves forward— toward the 'future'. It would also be possible to gloss this sign as **NEXT-WEEK.**

• *me*-**PARTICIPATE-IN**-*cntr*

This is an example of a verb which can indicate the subject and object by it's direction of movement. For further explanation and discussion, see Unit 4.

$$\overline{\hspace{3cm}\text{nodding}}$$
• **ME   RECEIVE-REGULARLY   D-A**

Here the Signer has chosen to use **D-A** to refer to the *Deaf American* instead of the signs **DEAF AMERICA**. Such abbreviations or acronyms are frequently used in ASL.

<pre>
                           nodding+brow raise   nod   (gaze rt   )
Pat₄: PARTICIPATE-IN-nad   FINISH,   CAN   GO-TO-rt   MEETING   EVERY-TWO-YEAR-FUTURE,
</pre>

Pat₄:

<pre>
         nodding+q
         RIGHT
</pre>

- **PARTICIPATE-IN-*nad***

    Notice that the sign **PARTICIPATE-IN-*nad*** is signed in the same general location in which the previous Signer placed the **NAD.** This is because generally when something has been established in a particular location, other Signers in the conversation will use that location if they also want to talk about that thing. For more information on verbs like **PARTICIPATE-IN-____** , see Unit 4.

<pre>
         nodding   nodding   t
Lee₄: ME   GO-TO-lf   ONCE-IN-AWHILE,   "UMMM"   TWO-YEAR-FUTURE,

         ME   GO-TO-lf
</pre>

<pre>
         nodding   _____ nodding
  •   ME   GO-TO-lf   ONCE-IN-AWHILE,
</pre>

    Notice that the Signer begins responding affirmatively to Pat's question by nodding before beginning to sign. Notice also that the direction of the sign **GO-TO-*lf*** is toward the same location used by Pat in discussing the meetings every two years.

- **ONCE-IN-AWHILE**

    The time sign **ONCE-IN-AWHILE** indicates that an event occurs periodically. This sign can also be moved along the time line to indicate whether the periodic occurrence existed in the past and will continue in the future or whether it will start at some future date.

<pre>
                              t
  • TWO-YEAR-FUTURE
</pre>

    Notice that this sign occurs with the non-manual behaviors described in Unit 1 to indicate a topic. This sign also illustrates how a number handshape (**TWO**) can be incorporated into a time sign. Compare the illustration of this sign with the illustration for **EVERY-TWO-YEAR-FUTURE** and notice the difference in movement between the two signs. The addition of fast repeated movement adds the idea of regularity to the sign **TWO-YEAR-FUTURE.**

- **ME   GO-TO-*lf***

    Again notice that the direction of the sign **GO-TO-*lf*** is consistent with the first use of this sign.

Pat₅:
                                                                           wh-q
TWO-YEAR-FUTURE, WHYwg

Notice that the non-manual behaviors used for 'wh-word' questions occur throughout the entire sentence. These behaviors are described in Unit 1.

There are certain variants (other forms) of the sign **WHY** which are commonly seen. Two of the variants for the sign are illustrated below. Notice that in both variants, some portion of the hand wiggles ('wg').

    WHY   **WHYwg**   **WHYwg**

                                                                         t
Lee₅: **THAT-ONE-*lf* TWO-YEAR-FUTURE, N-A-D (2h)THRILL ONE HUNDRED YEAR CELEBRATE**

- **THAT-ONE-*lf***

        This sign is used to refer to a particular person, place, or thing. In this case, because it is produced toward the location given to NAD conventions (to Lee's left and to Pat's right), it refers to the specific convention which will take place in two years.

- **(2h)THRILL**

        The manual portion of this sign is identical to the manual portion of the sign (2h)**WHAT'S-UP.** However, the non-manual (facial) behavior is somewhat different. Compare the following illustrations and note the different facial behaviors.

    (2h)THRILL   **(2h)WHAT'S-UP**

- ONE͡ HUNDRED

> This is another example of two signs which frequently occur together and 'flow together' in such a way that they seem more like a single sign. Unlike the joined signs **ONE͡ HUNDRED**, the signs **TWO-HUNDRED, THREE-HUNDRED, FOUR-HUNDRED,** and **FIVE-HUNDRED** keep the same handshape throughout the sign and are single signs. They are made by using the appropriate number handshape (**TWO, THREE, FOUR** or **FIVE**) and bending the fingers repeatedly at the middle joints, or bending the fingers once as the hand moves backward (toward the Signer).

H. Sample Drills

<u>   t   </u>

1. ONE-YEAR-PAST, ME   RECEIVE-REGULARLY,   STOP

   TWO-YEAR-PAST

   THREE-YEAR-PAST

   ONE-WEEK-PAST

   TWO-WEEK-PAST

   ONE-DAY-PAST

   TODAY

   TWO-MONTH-PAST

   THREE-MONTH-PAST

   ONE-WEEK-PAST

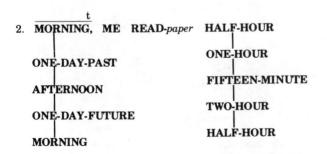

           <u>   t   </u>

2. MORNING, ME   READ-*paper*   HALF-HOUR

                                    ONE-HOUR

   ONE-DAY-PAST   FIFTEEN-MINUTE

   AFTERNOON

                                    TWO-HOUR

   ONE-DAY-FUTURE

                                    HALF-HOUR

   MORNING

```
              nodding+brow raise        (gaze rt                                      )  nodding+q
3. PARTICIPATE-IN-cntr  FINISH,  CAN  GO-TO-rt  MEETING  EVERY-TWO-YEAR-FUTURE,  RIGHT
                                                                  |
                                                         EVERY-YEAR-FUTURE
                                                                  |
                                                         ONE-YEAR-FUTURE
                                                                  |
                                                         THREE-YEAR-FUTURE
                                                                  |
                                                         ONE-WEEK-FUTURE
                                                                  |
                                                         TWO-WEEK-FUTURE
                                                                  |
                                                         ONCE-IN-AWHILE
                                                                  |
                                                         EVERY-THREE-YEAR-FUTURE
                                                                  |
                                                         EVERY-TWO-YEAR-FUTURE
```

I. Video Notes

If you have access to the videotape package designed to accompany these texts, you will notice the following:

- the use of the attention-getting, conversation opener "**HEY**" by the first Signer.

- several types of 'addressee feedback'—that is, the signals which the addressee (the non-signing participant) gives the Signer (while he is signing) to show understanding of the Signer's message. For English speakers, addressee feedback is often given through headnodding, specific facial behavior and the use of expressions such as 'Yeah', 'Uh-huh', 'Ahh', etc. In this dialogue, this feedback occurs via headnodding, facial behavior, and occasional body shifts forward toward the Signer.

- the non-manual behaviors used to ask 'yes/no' and 'wh-word' questions and to make negative statements.

Unit 3

Pronominalization

A. Synopsis

Pat and Lee meet on a street corner. Pat asks if Lee has seen the National Theatre of the Deaf (NTD) play. Lee replies that s/he and a friend △ₘ went last night. Pat asks if Lee saw △ᵦ . Lee says that s/he and △ᵦ went out to eat two days ago and talked about the play, summer school, and a number of other things. Pat says that last summer s/he went to the NTD summer school. Lee asks if Pat went alone. Pat replies that s/he drove there alone and when s/he got there, there were several deaf people that s/he knew. Lee asks if they were drama majors. Pat says that they were from community theatre groups such as the ones in Chicago and Washington, D.C.

B. Cultural Information: The National Theatre of the Deaf

The National Theatre of the Deaf (NTD) was started in 1966 at the Eugene O'Neill Memorial Theatre in Waterford, Connecticut. Although comprised mostly of Deaf professional actors and actresses, NTD does not perform solely for Deaf audiences. Rather, by using professional, hearing actors and actresses, NTD performs for mixed audiences of deaf and hearing people. NTD has toured all over the world and has performed for hundreds of thousands of people. A Tony Award was given to NTD for its outstanding contribution to the theatre, and several programs have appeared on national television (e.g. "A Child's Christmas in Wales" and "My Third Eye"). The company tours the U.S. every year in the Fall and Spring. In 1967, a summer school program was initiated to provide professional training opportunities to aspiring Deaf actors and actresses. The NTD summer school has been held annually ever since. In 1968, the Little Theatre of the Deaf (LTD) was formed. LTD is composed of a few members of the NTD company who tour (between NTD tours) with a special program aimed at children. Several notable individuals are former members of NTD: Bernard Bragg, Gil Eastman, Lou Fant, and Jane Norman, to name a few. For more information about NTD, contact: National Theatre of the Deaf, 305 Great Neck Road, Waterford, Connecticut 06385.

C. Dialogue

Pat

Pat₁: q
                    SEE FINISH N-T-D DRAMA
"UMMM"   *YOU*

Pat₂: q
        SEE △ₐ YOU

Pat₃: t
                KNOW-THAT ONE-YEAR-PAST SUMMER, N-T-D SUMMER SCHOOL,
"UMMM" ⟶

        ME GO-TO-*rt*

Pat₄: nodding   br
        MYSELF DRIVE+ ARRIVE-AT-*rt*,

                             (gaze rt   )
        SEE-*rt* INDEX-*arc-rt* DEAF SEVERAL INDEX-*arc-rt* THEREABOUTS-*rt*

                (gaze rt   )
        ME KNOW+ INDEX-*arc-rt*

Pat₅: neg   t
        "NO-NO", KNOW CITY DRAMA GROUP,

                                                             nodding
        THINK SAME-AS WASHINGTON D-C CHICAGO THAT THEREABOUTS-*rt*

Lee

Lee$_1$:
<u>nodding</u>
PAST‿NIGHT  US-TWO-*rt* GO-*rt*

Lee$_2$: TWO-DAY-PAST US-TWO-*cntr* GO-*rt* EAT CHAT,

DRAMA SUMMER SCHOOL VARIOUS-THINGS

Lee$_3$:
<u>   q</u>
YOURSELF ONLY-ONE-*you* GO-TO-*lf*

Lee$_4$:
<u>   (gaze lf   )   q</u>
DEAF INDEX-*arc-lf* DRAMA SPECIALTY-FIELD

Lee$_5$:
<u>   nodding</u>
OH-I-SEE++

D. Key Illustrations

Pat

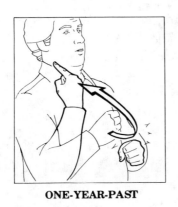

ONE-YEAR-PAST

THINK⏝SAME-AS

Lee

PAST⏝NIGHT

US-TWO-*rt*

GO-*rt*

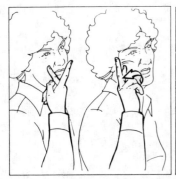

TWO-DAY-PAST

CHAT

VARIOUS-THINGS

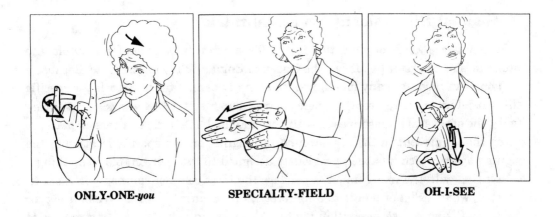

ONLY-ONE-*you*   SPECIALTY-FIELD   OH-I-SEE

E. Supplementary Illustrations

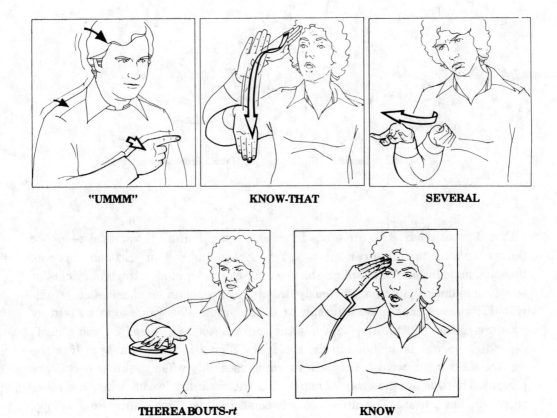

"UMMM"   KNOW-THAT   SEVERAL

THEREABOUTS-*rt*   KNOW

F. General Discussion: Pronominalization

Pronouns are words or signs that 'stand for' a noun. In English, for example, the pronoun 'she' can refer to 'Mary', 'the Queen of England', 'my mother', etc. Because a pronoun can have so many meanings, it generally cannot be used until the specific thing it refers to (its referent) is made clear. Pronouns in ASL are made by pointing (with one of several handshapes or with non-manual behaviors) to a person, place, or thing that is present in the area around the Signer, or to a specific location in the signing space which has been previously assigned to that person, place, or thing.

Pointing with the index finger is perhaps the most common 'pronoun' in ASL. In general, when a Signer points to him/herself, the meaning is 'I/me'. When a Signer points to the person s/he is talking with, the meaning is 'you'. Pointing to a third person means 'he/him' or 'she/her'. Pointing to a thing means 'it'. Pointing to a place (e.g. a building) means 'there', and pointing down to the 'ground' means 'here'.

Another, more formal, way of referring to a person is to use what can be called *honorific* referencing. This is often used in formal contexts such as in speeches, introductions, poetry, and drama. If accompanied by the appropriate facial expression, it can also be used as a sarcastic reference.

ME (honorific)   HIM/HER (honorific)

Plural pronouns in ASL are made in several ways. Pointing to several people or things one after the other can mean 'you, you, you, and you' or 'this one, this one, this one, and this one'. This might be used, for example, in selecting volunteers or selecting teams for a game. Obviously, this type of pronoun emphasizes each individual. However, the Signer can refer to all the people s/he wants to talk about by pointing to them in an arc. This has the meaning of 'they/them' or 'you-plural', depending on who is included in the arc. If the Signer includes him/herself in the arc, the meaning is 'we/us'. This latter form is used only when the other people are present. There is another way of expressing the meaning 'we/us' when the other people are not present. The difference between these two signs is illustrated below.

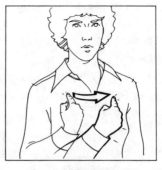

WE
(other people present)

WE
(other people not present)

When the Signer wishes to talk about two people or two things, s/he very often will use the handshape shown on the left or its variant on the right and move it back and forth between the two people.

For example, if the Signer wishes to refer to him/herself and a person to the right, this '2' handshape pronoun would be used, meaning 'us two'.

US-TWO-*rt*

The Signer can also use this sign to mean 'us two' (the Signer and the person s/he is talking with), 'those two', or 'you two' by moving the sign back and forth between the appropriate people or their assigned locations in space. While this pronoun can be used to refer to two people or two things, it cannot be used to refer to a person and a thing together.

Pronouns that mean 'myself', 'yourself', etc., are called *reflexive or emphatic* pronouns. The pronoun meaning 'myself' has two forms that are illustrated below.

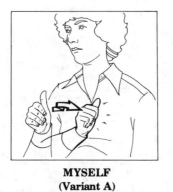

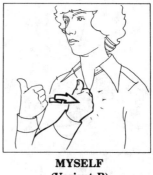

MYSELF
(Variant A)

MYSELF
(Variant B)

Singular reflexive/emphatic pronouns (like 'yourself', 'himself', or 'itself') are expressed by moving this handshape toward the person or thing with a repeated shaking movement. Thus, the Signer 'points' with this handshape (specifically with the area between the knuckles and first finger joint) to the person or thing. In the case of plurals ('yourselves' or 'themselves'), this pronoun also uses an arc like the one described above. If the Signer wishes to include him/herself in the group being referenced, s/he may use the sign **OURSELVES** (illustrated below). If the other members of the group are present, the Signer may use the sign **YOURSELVES-AND-MYSELF** to convey the meaning 'ourselves'.

OURSELVES   **YOURSELVES-AND-MYSELF**

It is relatively easy to refer to people or things that are present in the immediate communication area by simply pointing to them. However, when the people or things are *not* present in the immediate environment, then the Signer must 'set up' or 'establish' these non-present people or things in specific locations in the signing space. The Signer can then point to those locations which 'stand for' certain people or things. These points serve as pronouns—just as if the people or things were really there. Most nouns (e.g. 'my brother', 'New York', 'a tree', 'my class') can be and most often are given a specific location if the Signer wishes to refer back to them.

There are several strategies that Signers use to set up or assign specific spatial locations. If the Signer is talking about an event in the past in which people or things were arranged in specific places (or in a specific order), then the Signer will set them up in the places that reflect where they really were. This "reality principle" is similar to the principle of pointing to people or things that are actually present. The Signer visualizes in his/her mind the actual arrangement of people or things. Then, by using the space around his/her body, the Signer re-creates that arrangement.

Obviously, if the Signer doesn't know the exact location or arrangement of people or things, then the "reality principle" can't be followed. Instead, many right-handed Signers will set up the first person or thing they want to talk about on their right — in the area between the Signer and the person s/he is talking with (Fig. 3.1). If another person or thing is set up, it usually will be located in the area on the Signer's left (Fig. 3.2). Additional people or things can also be located in the signing space. The exact location will depend upon the relationship between the persons or things each location represents and when they occur in the narrative. For example, if the Signer is describing a situation in which two girls are talking to their father, the two girls might be given locations to the right and the father given a location to the left (Fig. 3.3).

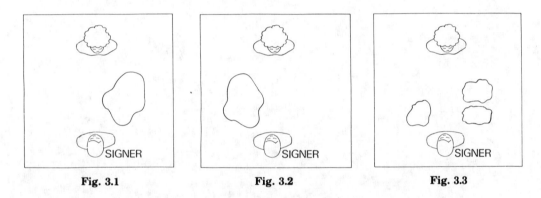

Fig. 3.1   Fig. 3.2   Fig. 3.3

The following principles are also helpful in learning how to use spatial locations to represent people or things that are not present:

(a) Once a Signer has established a person, place, or thing (referent) in space, all other references to that person/place/thing should be to that same location *unless* the referent has clearly been moved to another location.

(b) Once a Signer has established a person, place, or thing in space, other Signers in the conversation will also make consistent use of that location when referring to the same person/place/thing.

(c) In narratives, it is helpful to think ahead and have a 'mental overview' of the various locations that will be used — much like an aerial photograph, or a map. This helps you 'see' the spatial relationships between different persons, places, or things.

aerial view   **Signer's perspective**

There are, of course, several other types of pronouns and ways to handle people, places, or things that are not present in the communication area. These will be discussed as they occur in other units.

G. Text Analysis

Pat₁: $\overline{\text{SEE͜ FINISH   N-T-D   DRAMA}}^{\text{q}}$
            "UMMM"   *YOU*

- $\overline{\text{SEE͜ FINISH   N-T-D   DRAMA}}^{\text{q}}$
                                        YOU

  Notice that the Signer uses the non-manual 'q' signal to show that this sentence is a question (see Unit 1). Also notice that the Signer ends the question by pointing to the other person—YOU. As was mentioned in Unit 1, this is very common at the end of a question.

- SEE͜ FINISH

  The sign SEE͜ FINISH is a combination of the signs SEE and FINISH (made with one hand). However, these two signs flow together in such a way that they appear to be a single sign. When two signs flow together like this, they are glossed in this text with the symbol ͜ . Often there are changes in one or both signs which help them flow together. Other instances of signs like this will be discussed in future units.

Lee₁: $\overset{\text{nodding}}{\overline{\text{PAST͜ NIGHT   } \triangle_M \text{   US-TWO-}rt \text{   GO-}rt}}$

- nodding

  Notice that Lee has answered Pat's question by nodding even before starting to sign.

- PAST͜ NIGHT

  The sign PAST͜ NIGHT is another example of a sign like SEE͜ FINISH. Look at the illustration and notice how the signs PAST and NIGHT have changed slightly so that they flow together.

- $\triangle_M$

  The sign $\triangle_M$ is another example of a name sign in ASL. In most cases, Deaf persons are given their name signs in residential schools by their peers. These name signs are quite often retained for a person's entire life. If a woman's name sign is an initialized form of her maiden name, she generally will not change that name sign even though her legal, English name may change.

- US-TWO-*rt*

  US-TWO-*rt* is a pronoun that refers to two people or two things. Here the Signer is referring to him/herself and $\triangle_M$. The same sign is used with a different meaning later on in this dialogue.

Pat₂: $\overline{\text{SEE } \underset{\text{\tiny B}}{\triangle} \text{ YOU}}^{\text{q}}$

      • $\underset{\text{\tiny B}}{\triangle}$

> Another interesting note about name signs is that they can be and often are used to tease or insult a person by slightly changing the way the sign is produced. For example, a possible name sign for Victor ('V' tap index finger on the temple) might be changed when teasing someone by signing it as 'V' tap back of hand on forehead (signing STUPID). Such teasing and insulting is, of course, more common among children.

Lee₂: **TWO-DAY-PAST US-TWO-*cntr* GO-*rt* EAT CHAT,**

      DRAMA SUMMER SCHOOL VARIOUS-THINGS

      • **TWO-DAY-PAST**

> This is another example of a time sign which sets the tense for the remainder of the Signer's utterance. Notice in the illustration that the Signer's facial expression conveys the meaning 'just' or 'recently'.

      • **US-TWO-*cntr***

> This use of the pronoun means '$\underset{\text{\tiny A}}{\triangle}$ and I'. Since the previous Signer (Pat) had located $\underset{\text{\tiny A}}{\triangle}$ in neutral space, Lee maintained that location in his/her use of this pronoun.

Pat₃: $\overline{\hphantom{xxxxx}\text{KNOW-THAT ONE-YEAR-PAST SUMMER, N-T-D SUMMER SCHOOL,}}^{\text{t}}$
"UMMM" ————→

    ME GO-TO-*rt*

       • **ONE-YEAR-PAST**

> This is another example of a time sign which the Signer uses to establish a new time frame for what is to follow. Unless the other Signer introduces a new time frame, all further conversation is understood to relate to ONE-YEAR-PAST. Another way to make this sign is shown below.

ONE-YEAR-PASTwg

- **ME**

> This is an example of a 'first person' pronoun. The Signer is called the 'first person'. The person s/he is talking with is called the 'second person'. Any other person, place, or thing is called the 'third person'.

- **GO-TO-*rt***

> This is an example of a verb which can indicate its subject and/or object by moving to or from specific locations. Further explanation is given in Unit 4. The Signer sets up the NTD summer school to the right by moving the verb toward that location. The other Signer recognizes this when s/he later signs GO-TO-*lf*.

Lee$_3$: $\overline{\text{\textbf{YOURSELF} \quad \textbf{ONLY-ONE-}\textit{you} \quad \textbf{GO-TO-}\textit{lf}}}^{\text{q}}$

- **YOURSELF**

> This is an example of a reflexive pronoun. In this situation, it would also have been appropriate for the Signer to use the sign **YOU**.

- **ONLY-ONE-*you***

> This is an example of a sign which can be moved to a particular location to show who or what it refers to. Note the difference between the sign **ONLY-ONE-*you*** (illustrated above) and the sign **ONLY-ONE-*me*** illustrated here.

ONLY-ONE-*me*

- **GO-TO-*lf***

> Notice that the direction of this sign is to Lee's left. Thus, Lee uses the same location that was established by Pat for the NTD summer school.

nodding   br

Pat₄:
<u>nodding</u>   <u>   br   </u>

MYSELF   DRIVE+   ARRIVE-AT-*rt*,

                                    (gaze rt   )

SEE-*rt*   INDEX-*arc-rt*   DEAF   SEVERAL   INDEX-*arc-rt*   THEREABOUTS-*rt*

          (gaze rt   )

ME   KNOW+   INDEX-*arc-rt*

> <u>nodding</u>
> - **MYSELF**
>
>> Notice that the Signer has responded affirmatively to the question by nodding while producing the sign **MYSELF**. This sign (**MYSELF**) is an example of a reflexive pronoun in ASL.
>
> - **ARRIVE-AT-*rt***
>
>> Notice that the sign **ARRIVE-AT-*rt*** is produced to the right—the same location that had been assigned to the summer school by the verb **GO-TO-*rt***. Notice also that the signs **SEE-*rt*, INDEX-*arc-rt*,** and **THEREABOUTS-*rt*** are all produced to the right since they all refer to the summer school or to people who were at the summer school.
>
> (gaze rt   )
> - **INDEX-*arc-rt***
>
>> The use of **INDEX-*arc-rt*** is an example of a plural pronoun which refers to the Deaf people at the summer school. Note that this sign is accompanied by a gaze to the right. Thus, the Signer's direction of eye gaze also 'agrees with' the location of the school and people.

          (gaze lf   )   q

Lee₄: **DEAF   INDEX-*arc-lf*   DRAMA   SPECIALTY-FIELD**

> - **DEAF**
>
>> There are several variants of this sign and at least one formal sign with this meaning. Compare the two illustrations below.

DEAF   DEAF
(formal)

                 (gaze lf   )
- **INDEX**-*arc-lf*

> Notice that the Signer maintains the original spatial lo-
> cation that was assigned to the summer school—to Pat's
> right and to Lee's left. Notice also that an arc is used since
> the referent is plural (several), and that the Signer's eye
> gaze toward the left also 'agrees with' the location of the
> summer school.

                     neg   t

Pat₅: **"NO-NO", KNOW CITY DRAMA GROUP,**

                                                         nodding
THINK SAME-AS WASHINGTON D-C CHICAGO THAT THEREABOUTS-*rt*

                    neg
- **"NO-NO"**

> This gesture is made by shaking one or both open hands
> back and forth (palms facing outward). Another gesture
> with the same meaning is made by shaking the index
> finger(s) back and forth. Notice that the gesture is accom-
> panied by the non-manual behaviors for negation that are
> described in Unit 1.

                                      t
- **KNOW CITY DRAMA GROUP**

> Notice that this entire phrase is the 'topic' of the sentence.
> (See Unit 1 for a description of the non-manual behaviors
> used to signal 'topics'.)
>
>   The sign **GROUP** is interesting because the sign can be
> changed to indicate either a small group or a large group.
> This is done by changing the distance between the two
> hands and by spreading the fingers to indicate a large
> group.

GROUP   GROUP
(relatively small)   (relatively large)

• THINK⏜SAME-AS

> This is another example of two signs which are frequently
> used together. When used together, they mean 'like', 'just
> like', 'the same as', or 'for example'.

H. Sample Drills

1. <u>nodding</u>

PAST⏜NIGHT △ⓜ   US-TWO-*rt*   GO-*rt*

ONE-WEEK-PAST

ONE-WEEK-FUTURE

TWO-DAY-PAST

ONE-YEAR-PAST

TWO-YEAR-FUTURE

ONE-YEAR-PAST

TWO-WEEK-PAST

PAST⏜NIGHT

2. TWO-DAY-PAST US-TWO-*cntr* GO-*rt* EAT CHAT, DRAMA SUMMER SCHOOL VARIOUS-THINGS

US-TWO-*rt*   STATE-SCHOOL

OURSELVES   #JOB

YOURSELVES-AND-MYSELF   MEETING

INDEX-*arc-lf*   DEAF   AMERICA

US-TWO-*cntr*   DRAMA

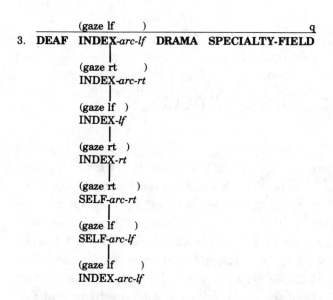

```
            (gaze lf      )                                              q
3.  DEAF  INDEX-arc-lf  DRAMA  SPECIALTY-FIELD
              |
            (gaze rt      )
            INDEX-arc-rt
              |
            (gaze lf  )
            INDEX-lf
              |
            (gaze rt  )
            INDEX-rt
              |
            (gaze rt     )
            SELF-arc-rt
              |
            (gaze lf     )
            SELF-arc-lf
              |
            (gaze lf      )
            INDEX-arc-lf
```

I. Video Notes

If you have access to the videotape package designed to accompany these texts, you will notice the following:

- Lee signs **ONE-DAY-PAST͡NIGHT** instead of **PAST͡NIGHT**. The sign **ONE-DAY-PAST** is often glossed as **YESTERDAY**. However, since it is often used in combination with the signs **MORNING** and **NIGHT** to mean 'the next morning' and 'the night before', it seems more appropriate to gloss it as **ONE-DAY-PAST**. The sign **ONE-DAY-FUTURE** (often glossed as **TOMORROW**) also occurs in combination with **MORNING** and **NIGHT** with the meanings 'the next morning' and 'the next night'.

- The name signs Ⓐ and Ⓑ are made over the heart which is a common location for name signs.

- In Pat's fourth turn (... **SEVERAL   INDEX-arc-rt THEREABOUTS-rt ME   KNOW + ...**) the sign **ME** is not made with the index finger. Rather, it is made with an open handshape because of the influence of the sign before it (**THEREABOUTS-rt**) and the sign after it (**KNOW +**)—both of which use an open handshape.

- The signs **CHAT** (Lee$_2$) and **DRIVE +** (Pat$_4$) occur with a particular non-manual facial behavior which conveys the meaning 'regularly', 'normally', or 'not out of the ordinary'.

- The signs **ONE-DAY-PAST͡NIGHT** (Lee$_1$) and **TWO-DAY-PAST** (Lee$_2$) occur with a non-manual facial behavior which conveys the idea of 'closeness in space or time'.

Unit 4

Subjects and Objects

A. Synopsis

Pat and Lee are at a restaurant and Pat asks if Lee's parents are deaf. Lee says that his/her whole family is deaf—two brothers, a sister, and both parents. Lee then asks if Pat's parents are deaf. Pat says that they are hearing. Pat also has a sister and a brother who are hearing. Lee asks how Pat became deaf. Pat doesn't know and neither does his/her mother. It seems that his/her mother was affected by some medication. Lee asks if a doctor gave the medication to Pat's mother. Pat says that his/her mother got sick and went to the hospital where the doctor examined her quite thoroughly for some time. Then the doctor gave her some medicine and she went home. Later Pat was born deaf. Lee asks if Pat's parents sign. Pat says that they don't because the doctor told them not to sign and that developing Pat's oral skills was important and better than signing. Lee responds that the doctor is really silly and knows nothing about deafness.

B. Cultural Information: Causes of Deafness

When examining the factors that cause deafness (i.e. the etiology of deafness), it is useful to look at three general categories: factors prior to birth, factors during the time of birth, and factors during childhood, adolescence, and adulthood. Deafness prior to birth (*congenital deafness*) is generally due to one of two causes—heredity or rubella. Heredity, or genetic factors, has been the leading cause of deafness in the twentieth century, except during rubella epidemics. In fact, approximately 50–60% of all deafness can be attributed to genetic factors. There are approximately 55 known forms of genetic deafness; ten of these also involve both hearing loss and visual difficulties. The second cause of congenital deafness is rubella. The most recent epidemic of rubella in the U.S. was between 1963 and 1965. Rubella is usually responsible for 10% of the instances of congenital deafness. However, during this epidemic, the percent increased to approximately 50%. In addition to deafness, rubella can also cause visual problems and heart defects.

Prematurity and blood type incompatibility are the most frequent causes of deafness during the time of birth (the perinatal period). Approximately four times more deaf children than non-deaf children are born prematurely. Factors such as loss of oxygen and cerebral hemorrhage (which can cause damage to the nervous system) are more common among premature babies than full-term babies. Rh blood type incompatibility is the second cause of *perinatal deafness*. In such cases, the newborn baby is severely jaundiced. In such a condition, death may result. Of those babies who survive, a high proportion are deaf.

After the perinatal period, there are several other potential causes of deafness. In later childhood, meningitis and encephalitis may cause deafness. About 10% of deafness in children is caused by meningitis—which is an inflammation of the protective coverings of the brain and spinal cord. Deafness can also occur if virus-causing mumps, measles, etc., infect the brain and cause encephalitis. Additionally, there are other adventitious causes of deafness, such as damage to the auditory nerve or eardrum caused by putting foreign objects in the ear, sudden loud noises, or blows to the skull.

A very common distinction which is used in discussing the onset of deafness is whether a person was prelingually or postlingually deafened. This refers to whether or not deafness occurred before or after the acquisition of a language. In the past, however, ASL was not recognized as a language and this distinction only referred to the acquisition of spoken English. Thus, many Deaf children who were native users of ASL (i.e. they had Deaf parents and they knew ASL) were incorrectly categorized as prelingually deafened because they did not know English.

C. Dialogue

Pat

$$\overline{\hspace{5cm}q}$$
Pat₁: "UMMM", MOTHER FATHER DEAF YOU

$$\overline{\hspace{0.5cm}\text{neg}}$$
Pat₂: "NO-NO", HEARING, BROTHER SISTER SAME HEARING

$$\overline{\hspace{2cm}\text{neg}}\quad\overline{\hspace{1cm}\text{t}}\quad\overline{\hspace{1.5cm}\text{neg}}$$
Pat₃: "WELL" NOT-KNOW, MY MOTHER, NOT-KNOW INDEX-*lf,*

(gaze lf   ) _____neg_____
me-ASK-TO-*mother,*   NOT-KNOW INDEX-*mother,*

SEEM MEDICINE INFLUENCE-*mother* SEEM+

nodding   _____t_____
Pat₄: PAST MOTHER, BECOME-SICK, INDEX-*mother* FROM-*lf*-GO-TO-*rt* HOSPITAL,
                                                              INDEX-*rt,*

DOCTOR (2h)alt.SEARCH-*mother* INVESTIGATE-*mother*++, MEDICINE *doctor*-GIVE-TO-*mother,*

_____br___ (gaze lf   )   _____t_____
FINISH, FROM-*hospital*-GO-TO-*lf* HOME ,   FUTUREwg, ME BORN DEAF
                             INDEX-*lf,*   "WELL"

_____neg_____   (gaze lf)t
Pat₅: SIGN (2h)"NO-NO", DOCTOR *doctor*-TELL-TO-*lf,* SIGN, *doctor*-SAY-#NO-TO-*lf,*

IMPORTANT ORAL+ BETTER*, "WELL"

Lee

Lee₁:
                    _____nodding_____   _____t_____   _____t_____

       MOTHER FATHER DEAF, BROTHER-*lf* TWO-*lf*, DEAF, SISTER-*rt* ONE-*rt*, DEAF,

                                                           _____q_____

       #ALL-*arc* DEAF, YOUR MOTHER FATHER DEAF YOU

Lee₂:
                                _____wh-q_____

       HOW HAPPEN DEAF HOWwg

Lee₃:
                _____t_____ (nodding_____)q

       MEDICINE, DOCTOR *doctor*-GIVE-TO-*mother*

Lee₄:
                                _____q_____

       YOUR MOTHER FATHER SIGN

Lee₅:
       DOCTOR SILLY*, KNOW-NOTHING DEAF KNOW-NOTHING*

D. Key Illustrations

Pat

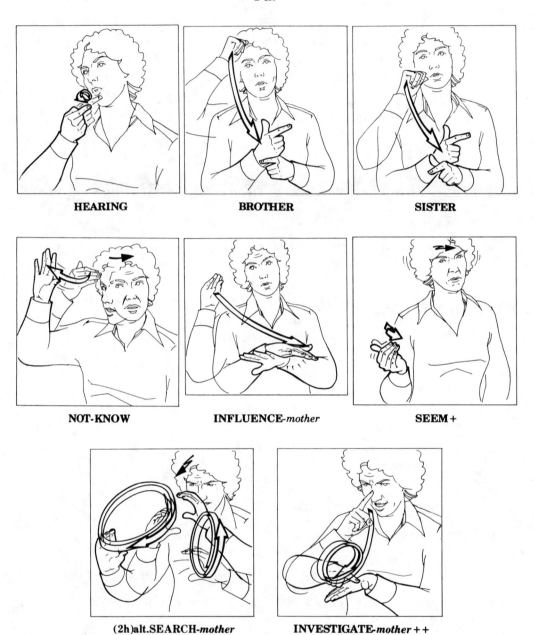

HEARING   BROTHER   SISTER

NOT-KNOW   INFLUENCE-*mother*   SEEM+

(2h)alt.SEARCH-*mother*   INVESTIGATE-*mother*++

Lee

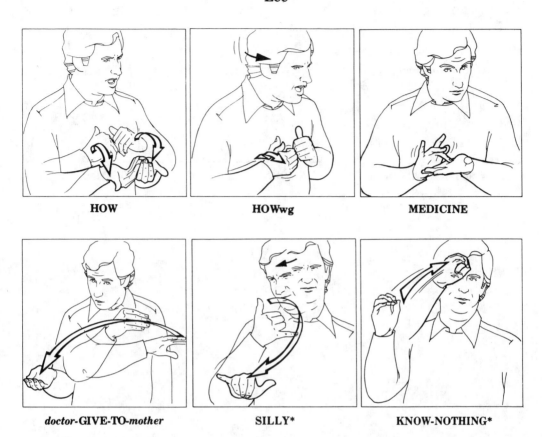

HOW   HOWwg   MEDICINE

doctor-GIVE-TO-*mother*   SILLY*   KNOW-NOTHING*

E. Supplementary Illustrations

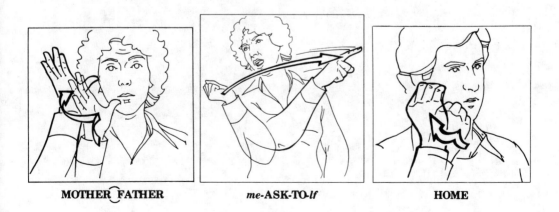

MOTHER◯FATHER   *me*-ASK-TO-*lf*   HOME

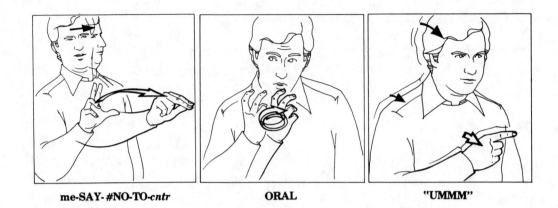

me-SAY-#NO-TO-*cntr*   **ORAL**   **"UMMM"**

F. General Discussion: Subjects and Objects

ASL has several ways to show who or what is the subject of a sentence and who or what is the object. One major way to do this involves changing the way the verb is made. This change in the form of the verb is called a *modulation,* and usually involves changing the direction of movement and/or the location of the verb. Thus, these modulations use the space around the Signer's body to indicate who or what is the subject or object.

To understand this use of the signing space, you need to understand that the spatial location of the Signer is 'first person', the location of the person the Signer is talking with is 'second person', and the spatial location of other people, places, or things is 'third person'. Many verbs in ASL use these locations to show who is doing something (the subject), or who is receiving that action (the direct or indirect object), or where the action occurs (the oblique object). By using these locations (i.e. by changing the direction of the sign from one location to another) with certain verbs in ASL, the Signer can express the meanings 'I ____ you', 'I ____ him/her', 'You ____ me', 'you ____ him/her', 'S/he ____ me', and 'S/he ____ you'.

Consider the verb ____-GIVE-TO- ____ , which is illustrated below:

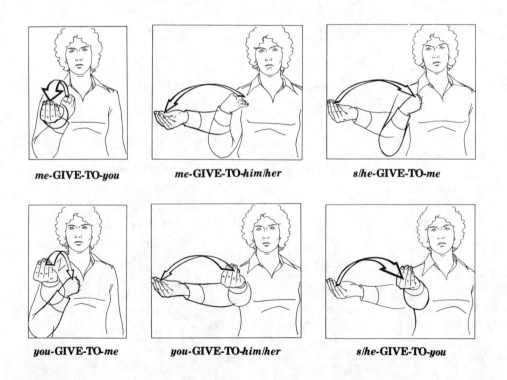

me-GIVE-TO-*you*	*me*-GIVE-TO-*him/her*	*s/he*-GIVE-TO-*me*
you-GIVE-TO-*me*	*you*-GIVE-TO-*him/her*	*s/he*-GIVE-TO-*you*

To express the meaning 'you give me', the verb moves from the subject (you) toward the object (me). That is, the verb moves from the 'second person' location to the 'first person' location. Likewise, to express the meaning 'I give you', the sign moves from the Signer (the subject) to the second person (the object). Then, assuming that the 'third person' is located to the Signer's right, the sign *me*-**GIVE-TO-**

him/her moves from the Signer's location to the location on the right. If that person was located to the Signer's left, then the verb would move from the Signer to the left.

Notice that with the verb ____-GIVE-TO-____ (and with other verbs of this type), there is no form which means simply 'to give', because every form of the verb indicates both a subject and an object. Often the sign *me*-**GIVE-TO**-*you* is illustrated in Sign Language texts but is simply glossed as **GIVE**. This fails to capture the vital fact that ASL verbs like ____-**GIVE-TO**-____ convey specific information about the subject and object of the verb. Verbs of this type have been called *directional verbs* because they can change their direction of movement to show who or what is the subject and/or object.

With some directional verbs which are made with both hands, the non-dominant hand (the left hand for a right-handed Signer) is held in a particular location and the palm orientation of the moving, dominant hand indicates the subject and object. For example, the non-dominant hand in the sign ____-**FLATTER**-____ is held in a particular location and the palm orientation of the moving, dominant hand indicates who is doing the flattering (the subject) and who is being flattered (the object).

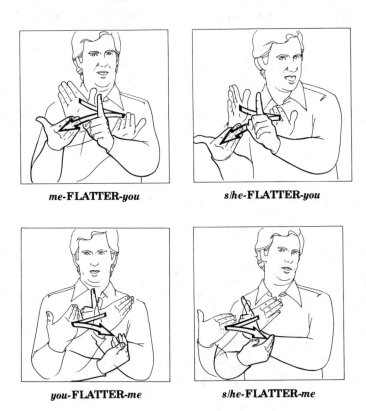

me-**FLATTER**-*you*   *s/he*-**FLATTER**-*you*

you-**FLATTER**-*me*   *s/he*-**FLATTER**-*me*

Obviously, in order to fully understand the meaning of such directional verbs, a person must first know what persons, places, or things have been given a location in space and where they have been located. Thus, if the Signer has established the location for a particular person to his/her right (e.g. ⓐ -rt) and then produces the sign ____-GIVE-TO-____ so that it moves from the right toward the Signer, the meaning is 'Pat gives me' (assuming that ⓐ is the name sign for 'Pat').

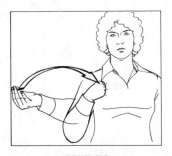

pat-GIVE-TO-me

Since these positions in space can also represent actual locations (e.g. 'San Francisco', 'your house'), some directional verbs indicate actual movement from one location to another location. For example, if the Signer establishes 'San Francisco' to his/her right and then signs **FROM-____-FLY-TO-____** from that location toward the Signer, it has the meaning 'from San Francisco fly to here'. If the Signer reverses the direction of movement so that the sign moves from the Signer toward the right, it has the meaning 'from here fly to San Francisco'. With a verb like **FROM-____-FLY-TO-____** or a verb like **FROM-____-GO-TO-____**, it is important that the specific locations be clearly identified by the Signer or be obvious from the context so that the meaning of the verb is clear.

FROM-*san francisco*-FLY-TO-*here*   **FROM-*here*-FLY-TO-*san francisco***

ASL has another set of verbs which use a specific location on the Signer's body to indicate where some action occurs (e.g. push on the shoulder). The location of these verbs will vary depending on which area of the body is involved. This use of a specific body location can be seen with verbs such as **BITE-(ON)-____**, **WASH-(AT)-____**, and **PUSH-(ON)-____**. For example, by changing the location of the sign **SHAVE-____**, the Signer can indicate which part of the body s/he is referring to.

SHAVE-*head*   **SHAVE-*face***   **SHAVE-*armpit***

This discussion has focused on a few ways that certain ASL verbs indicate who or what is the subject and/or object in a sentence. These ways include changing the verb's direction of movement, palm orientation, and/or location. Throughout this text, additional examples of verbs which indicate their subject and/or object will be noted and discussed.

G. Text Analysis

q
Pat₁: "UMMM", MOTHER FATHER DEAF YOU

- **MOTHER FATHER**

  This is another example of a sign in ASL in which two separate signs—**MOTHER** and **FATHER**—are produced together in such a way that they become like one sign. In fact, at some point in the future, it may be appropriate to gloss this sign as **PARENTS**.

- **DEAF**

  See Unit 3 for illustrations of variants of the sign **DEAF**.

nodding   t   t
Lee₁: MOTHER FATHER DEAF, BROTHER-*lf* TWO-*lf*, DEAF, SISTER-*rt* ONE-*rt*, DEAF,

q
#ALL-*arc* DEAF, YOUR MOTHER FATHER DEAF YOU

Notice that the Signer responds to the question Pat asks by nodding while signing. Notice also that in the segments dealing with the number of brothers and sisters, the noun (**BROTHER** or **SISTER**) and the number (**TWO** or **ONE**) are the topic of each sentence, and the adjective (**DEAF**) is the comment about each topic. Thus, these two sentences follow the order: noun-number-adjective.

- **SISTER-*rt***

  This sign (and the sign **BROTHER**) is an example of how two signs become a single sign. The two signs **FEMALE** and **SAME** have been used together to mean 'sister'. However, over time these two signs have blended together to form the single sign **SISTER**. This can be seen by comparing the two illustrations below.

SISTER   **SISTER**
(older form)   (newer form)

- **ONE**-*rt*

  Notice that the sign **ONE** is produced to the Signer's right side to 'agree with' the sign **SISTER** which is also produced to the right. The signs **TWO** and **BROTHER** are produced to the Signer's left side. This use of space helps to maintain clarity in a conversation and is very important if the Signer wishes to 'refer back' to his/her brothers or sister at some point later in the conversation.

- **#ALL**-*arc*

  This is an example of a fingerspelled loan sign. Notice that the sign is produced in an arc (moving from right to left) in front of the Signer, thus indicating that all of the family members are deaf (see Unit 3). This loan sign can also have several other movements. For example, to refer to all of the items on a list, the sign is produced with a downward movement.

- <u>   ^q</u>
  YOUR   MOTHER⁀FATHER   DEAF   YOU

  Notice that the Signer has tilted the head forward slightly and has raised his/her eyebrows during this question. This is the non-manual behavior which accompanies 'yes-no' questions in ASL (see Unit 1).

Lee₂: <u>   wh-q   </u>
      HOW   HAPPEN   DEAF   HOWwg

  Notice that the non-manual behaviors for 'wh-word' questions occur during the entire question. (See Unit 1 for a description of these behaviors.) Notice also that the Signer uses the sign **HOW** at the beginning and end of the question. However, when it appears at the end of the question, the variant **HOW**wg is used. Compare the illustrations of these two signs shown above.

Pat₃: <u>   neg   </u>   <u>   t   </u> <u>   neg   </u>
      "WELL"   NOT-KNOW,   MY   MOTHER,   NOT-KNOW   INDEX-*lf,*

      (gaze lf   )   <u>   neg   </u>
      me-**ASK-TO**-*mother,* **NOT-KNOW   INDEX**-*mother,*

      SEEM   MEDICINE   INFLUENCE-*mother* **SEEM +**

- <u>   neg   </u>
  NOT-KNOW

  This is an example of what has been called *negative incorporation*. This means that the sign is negated by adding an outward, twisting movement to the sign (in addition to the negative non-manual behaviors). Negative incorporation can also be seen in signs like:

NOT-LIKE   **NOT-WANT**

- **INDEX**-*lf*

    In this case, the **INDEX** is used to 'establish' or locate the Signer's mother to the left. This is important because the next sign uses this location to refer to the mother.

- *me*-**ASK-TO**-*mother*

    This is an example of a sign which, by its movement, indicates who is the subject and object. Since the sign moves from the Signer to the left (where 'mother' has been located), it is obvious that the Signer is asking the mother. If the movement of the sign was reversed (from the left to the Signer), then 'mother' would be asking the Signer.

- **INFLUENCE**-*mother*

    The movement of this sign is also toward the left to show that 'mother' is the object. This sign is made on the back of the non-dominant hand (in this case, the left hand). Sometimes Signers will move this hand to the left or right to be more exact in referring to a specific location.

Lee₃:
	t	(nodding	)q
MEDICINE,	DOCTOR	*doctor*-GIVE-TO-*mother*	

- <u>D</u>OCTOR

    This is an example of an *initialized* sign—a sign which has been influenced by English. The handshape in this sign is the same as the '**D**' handshape in the manual alphabet. Thus, the handshape corresponds to the first letter of the English gloss for that sign. Even though there is a non-initialized sign, DOCTOR, many Signers will use the initialized form, <u>D</u>OCTOR.

- *doctor*-**GIVE-TO**-*mother*

    Notice that the movement of this sign is from 'doctor' to 'mother' to show that the doctor is the subject, and the mother is the object. In this case, the sign moves to Lee's right because that is where Pat has established 'mother'. (Remember if Pat and Lee are facing each other, Pat's left is Lee's right). This sign illustrates how Signers will use previously established locations when they wish to refer to the same persons, places, or things.

Pat₄:
nodding   t
PAST MOTHER, BECOME-SICK, INDEX-*mother* **FROM**-*lf*-**GO-TO**-*rt* **HOSPITAL,**
                                                                            INDEX-rt,

DOCTOR (2h)alt.**SEARCH**-*mother* **INVESTIGATE**-*mother*++, MEDICINE *doctor*-**GIVE-TO**-*mother,*

        br   (gaze lf   )   t
FINISH, **FROM**-*hospital*-**GO-TO**-*lf* HOME   , FUTUREwg, ME BORN DEAF
                                  INDEX-lf,   *"WELL"*

- **FROM**-*lf*-**GO-TO**-*rt*

  Notice that again the Signer is being consistent with the use of space. 'Mother' had been located to the left and the Signer indicates that she went from there to somewhere else (located on the right). The next sign makes it clear that mother went to the 'hospital', which the Signer establishes to the right.

- **HOSPITAL**
  INDEX-rt

  Since the sign **HOSPITAL** is made by contacting the non-dominant upper arm, it is extremely awkward to try to set it up in space. Thus, the Signer uses the non-dominant hand to point to the location (on the right) which is then used to represent the hospital.

- (2h)alt.**SEARCH**-*mother*

  Again the Signer is consistently using spatial locations. 'Mother' has been 'moved' to the hospital on the right. This sign (which in this context means 'physical examination') is made toward the right to show that the doctor gave the mother a physical examination at the hospital.

- *doctor*-**GIVE-TO**-*mother*

  Since mother is still 'at the hospital', the sign moves to the Signer's right. Notice that the direction of movement is different than when Lee signed *doctor*-**GIVE-TO**-*mother* since mother was 'at home' (to Pat's left).

-        br
  FINISH

  As described in Unit 2, this sign usually indicates the completion of an action or event. Here the completion refers to the examination of the mother and giving her some medicine. When the sign **FINISH** occurs in this type of context, it is usually accompanied by a brow raise.

- (gaze lf   )
  FROM-*hospital*-**GO-TO**-*lf*

  With this sign, Pat clearly indicates that the mother left the hospital. The next sign makes it clear that the mother went 'home'.

Lee₄:
_____q
YOUR MOTHER FATHER SIGN

> Notice that the Signer has used the non-manual behaviors described in Unit 1 for asking 'yes-no' questions.

Pat₅:
```
            neg                           (gaze lf)t
SIGN  (2h)"NO-NO",  DOCTOR  doctor-TELL-TO-lf,  SIGN,    doctor-SAY-#NO-TO-lf,
```

IMPORTANT ORAL+ BETTER*, "WELL"

- *doctor-TELL-TO-lf*

  > Here again the Signer uses the direction of movement of the verb to indicate who is the subject and who is the object. The mother has been located to the Signer's left (and presumably the father, too, since this location has been identified with the sign **HOME**). So it is clear that the doctor told something to Pat's mother and father.

(gaze lf)t
- **SIGN,** *doctor-SAY-#NO-TO-lf,* **IMPORTANT ORAL+ BETTER*** "WELL"

  > Here the Signer is quoting the doctor. Generally in *direct address* statements (when quoting someone), the Signer will "role play" that person. In this case, the Signer gazes to the left, uses stress (**BETTER***), and a different body posture to 'become' the doctor. This strategy ('becoming' a person in order to quote them) is more common in ASL than in English.
  >
  > The sign _____-SAY-#NO-TO-_____ uses the fingerspelled loan sign #NO. But, because it can move from one location to another, it has the meaning 'say "no" to someone or something'.

Lee₅: DOCTOR SILLY*, KNOW-NOTHING DEAF KNOW-NOTHING*

- **DOCTOR**

  > Notice that here the Signer does not use the initialized form of the sign. Earlier in the dialogue, however, the same Signer did use the sign **DOCTOR.** This illustrates the fact that Signers can and do use older and newer forms of a sign even within the same conversation.

- **SILLY***

  > This is a stressed form of the sign **SILLY** which normally has repeated movement.

H. Sample Drills

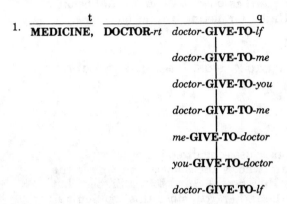

1.
$$\overline{}^{\,t} \quad \overline{}^{\,q}$$

MEDICINE,   DOCTOR-*rt*   *doctor*-**GIVE-TO**-*lf*

                             doctor-**GIVE-TO**-*me*

                             doctor-**GIVE-TO**-*you*

                             doctor-**GIVE-TO**-*me*

                             me-**GIVE-TO**-*doctor*

                             you-**GIVE-TO**-*doctor*

                             doctor-**GIVE-TO**-*lf*

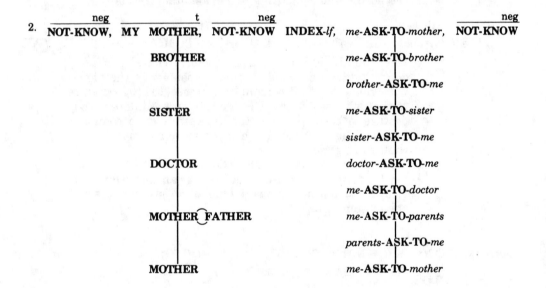

2.
$$\overline{}^{\,neg} \quad \overline{}^{\,t} \quad \overline{}^{\,neg} \qquad\qquad\qquad\qquad\qquad \overline{}^{\,neg}$$

NOT-KNOW,   MY   **MOTHER**,   NOT-KNOW   INDEX-*lf*,   *me*-**ASK-TO**-*mother*,   NOT-KNOW

              BROTHER   *me*-**ASK-TO**-*brother*

                                       brother-**ASK-TO**-*me*

              SISTER   *me*-**ASK-TO**-*sister*

                                       sister-**ASK-TO**-*me*

              DOCTOR   *doctor*-**ASK-TO**-*me*

                                       me-**ASK-TO**-*doctor*

              MOTHER◯FATHER   *me*-**ASK-TO**-*parents*

                                       parents-**ASK-TO**-*me*

              MOTHER   *me*-**ASK-TO**-*mother*

3.   **DOCTOR**-*rt*   *doctor*-**TELL-TO**-*lf*, $\overline{\text{SIGN,}}^{\,t}$ *doctor*-**SAY-#NO-TO**-*lf*

                    doctor-**TELL-TO**-*me*   *doctor*-**SAY-#NO-TO**-*me*

                    me-**TELL-TO**-*doctor*   *me*-**SAY-#NO-TO**-*doctor*

                    doctor-**TELL-TO**-*you*   *doctor*-**SAY-#NO-TO**-*you*

                    doctor-**TELL-TO**-*lf*   *doctor*-**SAY-#NO-TO**-*lf*

I. Video Notes

If you have access to the videotape package designed to accompany these texts, you will notice the following:

- Pat uses only one hand in signing most of the beginning portion of the dialogue. Often if a Signer is holding something in one hand (e.g. a book or cup), then s/he will use that object or the chest instead of the non-dominant or base hand for signs that normally require two hands.

- In Lee's first turn, the sign **#ALL**-*arc* is accompanied by "puffed cheeks"—a non-manual behavior that often means 'a lot' or 'a huge number of'.

- Accompanying the phrase <u>DOCTOR</u> *doctor*-**TELL-TO**-*lf* (Pat$_5$) is a non-manual signal which seems quite similar to the non-manual behaviors that accompany 'yes-no' questions. Actually, this signal is used to indicate a *rhetorical question* (a question the Signer asks but will immediately answer him/herself). In this case, the meaning is something like 'What did the doctor tell them? He said . . .'

- In general, notice the different types of non-manual feedback which Lee gives during the entire conversation: head nods, raised eyebrows, leaning forward, etc. This type of feedback is very important because it lets the Signer know that the other person is understanding and following the discussion.

Unit 5

Classifiers

A. Synopsis

Lee and Pat meet during their coffee break. Pat tells Lee that something awful happened last week. Lee wants to know what happened. Pat says that s/he had a car accident. Lee asks how it happened. Pat explains that s/he was stopped for a red light and was mulling over a few things in his/her mind. Suddenly this car came along and smashed into the driver's side of Pat's car. Lee asks if Pat was hurt. Pat says that s/he felt dizzy and it felt like his/her eyes were rolling around, but that went away after awhile. But the damage to the car was awful—the left rear was smashed in. Lee asks whether insurance will pay for the damage. Pat doesn't know because s/he hasn't sent in the premium check yet. Lee cringes a bit and asks whether Pat has had the car fixed yet. Pat says it was fixed yesterday and the bill was $800.

B. Cultural Information: Insurance and Deaf Drivers

A very common myth about deaf people is that they must be bad drivers because they can't hear. However, statistics and anecdotal data compiled by the National Association of the Deaf, the Department of Health, Education and Welfare, the U.S. Department of Transportation, and various state departments of motor vehicles show that this is not the case. In fact, these statistics show that, in general, deaf drivers tend to be better drivers than hearing drivers. According to the Department of Transportation, almost all driving decisions are made on the basis of sight, not sound (especially if the windows are up, the heater or air conditioner is on, and the radio is on). Thus, a deaf driver is functionally no different than a hearing driver in terms of making driving-related decisions. (In fact, automobile advertising frequently emphasizes the "quiet ride" and the ability of certain cars to eliminate outside noise).

The myth that deaf drivers are bad drivers made it somewhat difficult in the past for deaf drivers to obtain automobile insurance. In the past, most insurance companies felt that deaf drivers constituted a high-risk group. However, now there are approximately twenty-five major companies which provide deaf drivers with auto insurance. Thus, the "deaf-driver-bad-driver" myth is changing, and deaf drivers are now able to obtain reasonable insurance rates from reputable companies.

C. Dialogue

Pat

Pat₁:
    <u>   co   </u> <u>   t </u>
    "HEY",   **ONE-WEEK-PAST**,   **AWFUL**   **HAPPEN**

Pat₂:
    <u> t </u>
    CAR,   **ACCIDENT**

Pat₃:
               <u>   t   </u>   <u>   t   </u>
    "WELL"   **ME+,**   3→CL@*rt*'car', ⎯⎯⎯⎯⎯→   **ME**   3→CL'stop for light',
                                           RED͡ BURST-OF-light,⎯⎯⎯⎯⎯⎯⎯⎯⎯→

                                      (gaze lf,'surprised'   )   <u>   pow </u>
    ME   **MULL-OVER++,**   **UNEXPECTEDLY**   3→**CL**⎯⎯⎯⎯⎯⎯⎯⎯→
                                      3→*CL'car come from lf and smash into first car'*

Pat₄:
    <u>   nodding </u>
    (2h)alt.**DIZZY,**   **FEEL**   (2h)alt.F-CL'eyes rolling around',

    <u> t </u> <u> nodding </u> <u> t </u>
    LATER,   **DISSOLVE,**   **CAR,**   **AWFUL**   (2h)*left rear*-**SMASHED-IN**

Pat₅:
                                    <u>   t </u>
    NOT-KNOW,   **"WHY",**   **MONEY**   **RECT-CL**'check',   **NOT-YET**   **ME**   *me*-**SEND-TO**-*rt*

Pat₆:
    <u>   nodding </u> <u> (gaze at 'bill'   )br.raise </u>
    ONE-DAY-PAST   **FINISH,**   **#BILL**   **B-CL**'give me bill from rt'⎯⎯⎯⎯⎯→
                                             EIGHT   *HUNDRED*

Lee

Lee₁:
                                         wh-q
        (2h) #WHAT   (2h)"WHAT"

Lee₂:
                                        wh-q
        HOW   HAPPEN   HOWwg

Lee₃:
                                   q
        #HURT   YOU

Lee₄:
                                                     q
        INSURANCE PAY-TO-_you_   **RIGHT**

Lee₅:
                                                         q
        CAR   SEND-TO-_lf_ **#FIX   FINISH   YOU**

Lee₆:
        WOW

D. Key Illustrations

Pat

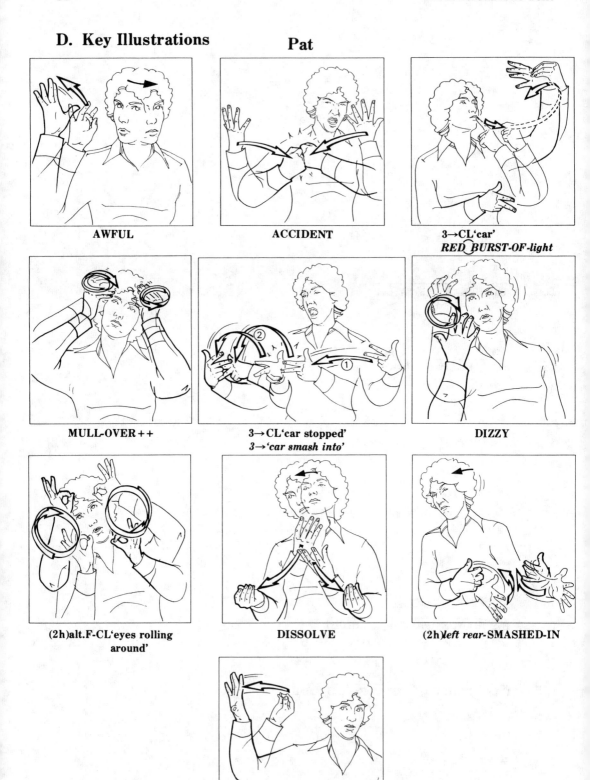

AWFUL

ACCIDENT

3→CL'car'
RED BURST-OF-light

MULL-OVER++

3→CL'car stopped'
3→'car smash into'

DIZZY

(2h)alt.F-CL'eyes rolling
around'

DISSOLVE

(2h)*left rear*-SMASHED-IN

me-SEND-TO-*rt*

Lee

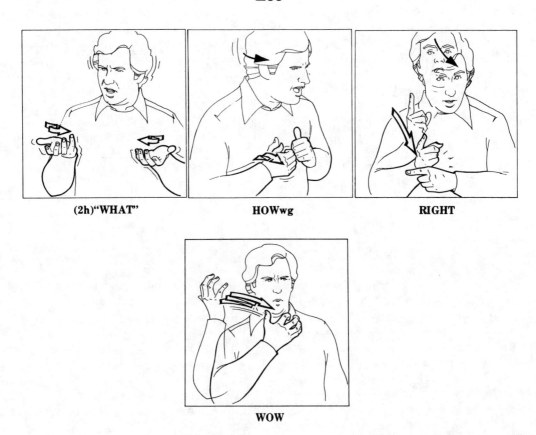

(2h)"WHAT"   HOWwg   RIGHT

WOW

E. Supplementary Illustrations

NOT-YET   FINISH   #WHAT

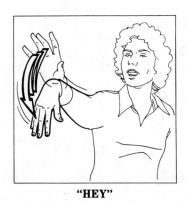

"HEY"

PAY-TO-*rt*

F. General Discussion: Classifiers

There is a fairly large set of signs in ASL which are called *classifiers*. These classifiers can be divided into two groups: (a) classifiers that are made with a particular handshape and that represent a noun and indicate the location and possible actions of that noun, and (b) classifiers that indicate something about the size, shape, texture, etc., of a noun as well as its location in space. These classifiers (b) are often made with two hands and are sometimes called *size and shape specifiers* (SASSes).

Some classifiers are like pronouns because they represent a particular group of nouns. Like pronouns, classifiers generally cannot be used until it is clear what they are representing. For example, the classifier 3→CL can represent things like a car, truck, bus, van, boat, or submarine. However, the Signer needs to indicate which one of these things s/he is talking about before using the classifier. Generally this is done by first signing the noun (e.g. **BOAT** or **#CAR**), and then using the classifier.

Below is a list of some of the classifiers in ASL and some of the nouns that they can represent.

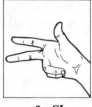

3→CL

car, bus, truck, van, boat, submarine

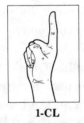

1-CL

person (e.g. boy, girl, man, woman)

1→CL

cigarette, pencil, rifle, log, pole (on its side), hot dog

B↓-CL

piece of paper, leaf, kite, bed

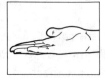

B↑-CL

book, piece of paper, pan

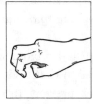

V:↓-CL

chair, person seated, (with
certain movements, also a snake,
cat, dog, or mouse)

V-CL

person standing (with alternating
finger movement, a person walking)

Some of the other classifiers will be described later in other units. As mentioned earlier, most classifiers give specific information about the location of the nouns they represent. For example, the 1-CL 'person' classifier can be placed to the Signer's right or left or directly in front of the Signer to show where a particular person was standing.

Many classifiers can also function as verbs. For example, if the 1-CL 'person' classifier moves toward the Signer, it has the meaning 'one person comes up to me'. If that person has already been identified (e.g. as 'Pat'), then the meaning is 'Pat comes up to me'. In addition, the classifier can show the direction of 'Pat's' movement. This is shown in the illustration below in which the Signer has already made it clear that the 1-CL classifier represents 'Pat'.

1-CL 'pat come up to me from right'

Further discussion of how classifiers give information about the location of the nouns they represent and their actions will be found in Unit 6. In addition to showing the locations and actions of people or things, classifiers can also show the 'manner' of an action (like adverbs in English). For example, the 1-CL 'person' classifier could have approached the Signer 'quickly' or 'slowly' or 'in a zig-zag fashion'.

The second type of classifiers (SASSes) can be used to more carefully and accurately describe the particular size, shape, depth, and/or texture of something (as well as give it a location in space). Thus, these classifiers are more like adjectives (although some are also used as pronouns). SASSes are used to describe nouns that share certain physical features (like 'flat and smooth' or 'thin and cylindrical'. For example, notice the common feature(s) that are shared by the nouns in the first list below (opposite the F-CL). Are they big? Are they flat? Are they rectangular? Are they circular? What are the common features shared by nouns in the second list (opposite the RECT-CL)?

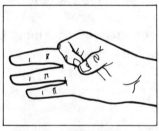

F-CL

coin, spot, eye, piece of
candy, poker chip, button, hole

RECT-CL

check, index cards, credit card,
bricks, tiles, invitation

The nouns described by the three classifiers illustrated below also share certain features. But notice how the handshape and the position of the hands shows that the 'poles' have very different sizes.

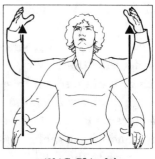

(2h)F-CL'pole'   (2h)L:-CL'pole'   (2h)C-CL'pole'

Obviously, the first is the smallest pole and the third is the largest. The difference in size is indicated not only by the choice of classifier but also by the different facial expressions which indicate the size (width) differences.

Certain handshapes can also be used to describe the shape of something. Generally, these handshapes 'trace' or 'outline' the shape of the thing.

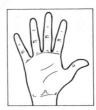
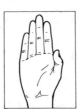

For example, suppose the Signer is talking about a table and does what you see in the illustration below. From this 'tracing' description, we know that the table is 'round' and is about 'medium' size.

1outline-CL'circular'

In the next illustration, the Signer is describing a surface that 'continues for a long distance' and appears to be 'smooth' or 'very even'. This classifier uses a variant of the **B-CL**, which is called the 'bent B' classifier, or **B:-CL**. Notice that the Signer's pursed lips and eye squint also emphasize the smooth, continuous nature of the surface.

(2h)B:-CL'smooth, continuous surface'

Classifiers can also be seen in more standard, commonly used signs in ASL, although they are generally not recognized as classifiers. For example, the 1-CL 'person' classifier occurs in signs which are often glossed as **MEET, HIT, FLATTER**, etc. Likewise, the signs which are glossed as **STAND, JUMP, FALL, GET-UP, SIT**, and **KNEEL** are made with common classifiers. Signs like **FENCE, CAGE, RAINBOW**, and **EYELASHES** use the '4' handshape classifier; signs like **FIRE, WAVES, TRAFFIC**, and **WAR** use the '5' handshape classifier. Notice again how each of these last two groups of nouns share common features.

Throughout the remaining units, many more classifiers will be illustrated and described. These descriptions will explore how classifiers are used to show, for example, the location, action, and number of various nouns. Further discussion of classifiers and their use will be found not only in the *General Discussion* sections but also in the *Text Analysis* sections.

G. Text Analysis

Pat₁:

    <u>co</u>   <u>   t   </u>

"HEY",   **ONE-WEEK-PAST, AWFUL HAPPEN**

-     <u>   co   </u>

  "HEY"

  This is an example of an attention-getting behavior which is frequently used by Signers to start or open a conversation. Notice that this conversational opener is made with the non-dominant hand.

-     <u>   t   </u>

  ONE-WEEK-PAST,

  This is an example of a time sign which moves backward on the "time line" to indicate a time in the past and which incorporates a number (**ONE**). See Unit 2 for further discussion.

- **AWFUL**

  This sign is often used to open or start a conversation or is used in the beginning of a conversation. The intent is to arouse the other person's curiosity to find out what is awful or terrible. Thus, this sign could have been used in place of **"HEY"**.

                        <u>   wh-q   </u>

Lee₁: (2h) **#WHAT** (2h)**"WHAT"**

- **(2h)#WHAT**

  This is another example of a fingerspelled loan sign in ASL. As with most fingerspelled loan signs, there is generally a deletion of some middle portion of the fingerspelled word. Also, the fingerspelled letters tend to flow together so that they look more like a sign.

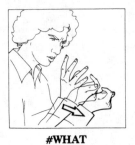 

         #WHAT   **WHAT**

#WHEN

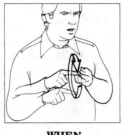

WHEN

Pat₃:
$$\overline{\text{ME+,}}^{\;t}\quad 3{\to}\text{CL@}rt\text{'car',}\xrightarrow[\underbrace{\text{RED BURST-OF}\text{-}\textit{light,}}]{\hspace{3cm}t}\!\!\longrightarrow \text{ME}\quad 3{\to}\text{CL'stop for light',}$$

"WELL"

ME MULL-OVER++,   UNEXPECTEDLY   (gaze lf,'surprised'   )   _____pow
3→CL ——————————————→
3→CL'car come from lf and smash into first car'

- **3→CL@**rt**'car',** $\xrightarrow{\hspace{2cm}t}$

  RED BURST-OF-_light_

  Notice that the meaning of the **3→CL** in this sentence is 'car' since the Signer has already indicated that what happened was a car accident. This classifier is held while the Signer uses the left hand to sign **RED BURST-OF-**_light_. The sign (**RED BURST-OF-**_light_) is a combination of the sign **RED** and a sign which is generally used to refer to lights or things which are lit up (sunlight, head-lights, flashing lights, etc.). However, the same sign is also used by some Signers to refer to other things like a shower, a dog's bark, or a sound from a loudspeaker.

- **UNEXPECTEDLY**

  This sign is related to the sign **WRONG**; however, the accompanying non-manual behaviors and the context give it the meaning 'unexpectedly' or 'by chance' or 'by accident'. Thus, we have chosen to gloss this as a separate sign.

- (gaze lf,'surprised'   )   pow
  3→CL ——————————————————→
  3→CL'car come from lf and smash into first car'

  Here the Signer 'holds' the position of the first car with the right hand **3→CL**. Then the Signer indicates that there was a second car by using a **3→CL** on the left hand. This use of both hands occurs frequently in ASL when the Signer wants to give specific information about the exact spatial relationship between two or more people, places, or things. (See Unit 6 for further discussion.) Notice here that if the Signer wanted to indicate that the second car came from the right side, then the left hand **3→CL** would be used to represent the car stopped at the light, and the right hand **3→CL** would be used for the second car.

Lee₃: $\overline{\text{#HURT\quad YOU}}^{\text{q}}$

- **#HURT**

  This is another example of a fingerspelled loan sign in ASL. This sign can be produced in different locations on the body to indicate what part of the body has been hurt. (See Unit 4 for other signs of this type and further discussion.) For example, to explain that the left shoulder has been hurt, a Signer might sign **#HURT** near or at the left shoulder.

#HURT-left shoulder

Pat₄: $\overline{\text{(2h)alt.}\textbf{DIZZY,}\quad\textbf{FEEL}}^{\text{nodding}}$ (2h)alt.**F-CL**'eyes rolling around',

$\overline{\text{LATER,}}^{\text{t}}\;\; \overline{\text{DISSOLVE,}\quad\text{CAR,}}^{\text{nodding}}\;\; \overline{\text{AWFUL}}^{\text{t}}$ (2h)*left rear*-**SMASHED-IN**

- (2h)alt.**F-CL**'eyes rolling around'

  It is clear that this classifier (**F-CL**) refers to the eyes— not only because of where the sign is made but also because of information given by the sign (2h)alt.**DIZZY**. The **F-CL** is the appropriate classifier here because eyeballs are 'small' and 'round'.

- (2h)*left rear*-**SMASHED-IN**

  Notice that the Signer produces this sign to the left and slightly to the rear. This sign describes what happened to the Signer's car in the accident—the other car (the left hand 3→CL) smashed into the left rear of the Signer's car (the right hand 3→CL). (See illustration and Unit 6 for further information.)

Lee₄: _____q
       INSURANCE PAY-TO-*you* RIGHT

- **PAY-TO-*you***

    This is another example of a verb which can indicate the subject and/or object by the direction of its movement. (See Unit 4 for further discussion of verbs of this type.) Notice also that the Signer uses the non-manual behaviors for asking a 'yes-no' question throughout this sentence. See Unit 1 for a description of these behaviors.

Pat₅: _____t
       NOT-KNOW, "WHY", MONEY RECT-CL'check', NOT-YET ME *me*-SEND-TO-*rt*

- **RECT-CL'check'**

    As discussed earlier, this classifier refers to things like credit cards, tiles, index cards, etc. In this context, it is clear that the meaning is 'check' because of the preceding sign **MONEY**.

- *me*-**SEND**-to-*rt*

    This is another example of a verb which can change its direction of movement to show who is the subject and who is the object. Further discussion of verbs like this can be found in Unit 4.

Pat₆: _____nodding_____   ____(gaze at 'bill'____)br.raise
       ONE-DAY-PAST FINISH,   #BILL   B-CL'give me bill from rt' ─────────→
                                                          EIGHT HUNDRED

- _____nodding_____
  ONE-DAY-PAST FINISH

    Notice that the Signer responds to Lee's question by nodding while adding additional information about when the car was fixed.

- ____(gaze at 'bill'____)br.raise
  #BILL   B-CL'give me bill from rt' ─────────→
                        EIGHT HUNDRED

    The 'B' handshape classifier (**B-CL**) generally represents a piece of paper or something that is flat. In this case, it is clear that it has the meaning 'bill' because of the previous fingerspelled loan sign **#BILL**. Notice that the **B-CL** can also function as a verb and can indicate its subject and object by the direction of movement. Here the movement is from the right toward the Signer. Thus, someone (presumably whoever fixed the car) gave the Signer a bill for $800. Notice that the Signer holds the 'bill' (the **B-CL**) and signs the amount of the bill with the left hand.

H. Sample Drills

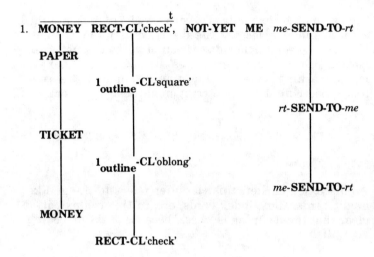

$$\overline{\hspace{3cm}}^{\,t}$$
1. **MONEY   RECT**-CL'check',   **NOT-YET   ME**   *me*-**SEND-TO**-*rt*

   PAPER

   1_{outline}-CL'square'

   rt-**SEND-TO**-*me*

   TICKET

   1_{outline}-CL'oblong'

   me-**SEND-TO**-*rt*

   MONEY

   RECT-CL'check'

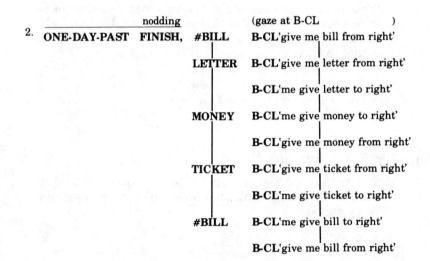

$$\overline{\hspace{3cm}}^{\,\text{nodding}}$$ (gaze at B-CL   )
2. **ONE-DAY-PAST   FINISH,   #BILL**   **B-CL**'give me bill from right'

   LETTER   **B-CL**'give me letter from right'

   B-CL'me give letter to right'

   MONEY   **B-CL**'me give money to right'

   B-CL'give me money from right'

   TICKET   **B-CL**'give me ticket from right'

   B-CL'me give ticket to right'

   #BILL   **B-CL**'me give bill to right'

   B-CL'give me bill from right'

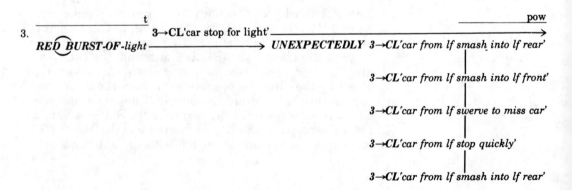

$$\overline{\hspace{2cm}}^{\,t}\hspace{4cm}\overline{\hspace{2cm}}^{\,\text{pow}}$$
3. $3{\rightarrow}$CL'car stop for light'
   RED BURST-OF-light ————————→ *UNEXPECTEDLY* $3{\rightarrow}$CL'car from lf smash into lf rear'

   $3{\rightarrow}$CL'car from lf smash into lf front'

   $3{\rightarrow}$CL'car from lf swerve to miss car'

   $3{\rightarrow}$CL'car from lf stop quickly'

   $3{\rightarrow}$CL'car from lf smash into lf rear'

I. Video Notes

If you have access to the videotape package designed to accompany these tapes, you will notice the following:

- The sign **MULL-OVER**++ (Pat$_3$) occurs with a particular facial behavior that conveys the meaning 'without paying attention' or 'carelessly'. This facial behavior also occurs with the sign (2h)alt.**F-CL**'eyes rolling around'.

- The gesture **"WHY"** (Pat$_5$) occurs with the non-manual signal that is used to indicate a *rhetorical question*. The Signer is not asking a real question here but is using this as a way to introduce new or additional information.

- Notice that Lee's portion of the dialogue provides some clear contrasts between the non-manual behaviors that occur with 'yes-no' questions and those that occur with 'wh-word' questions. Compare the descriptions of these behaviors (Unit 1) with Lee's performance in this dialogue.

In general, notice the versatility of classifiers in this dialogue. They can function as pronouns (3→**CL, RECT-CL, B-CL**), and/or as verbs (3→**CL**'car come from lf and smash into car', (2h)alt.**F-CL**'eyes rolling around', **B-CL**'give me bill from rt'). Also notice how classifiers can be used to provide information about the location or relationship between two things (e.g. two cars).

Unit 6

Locatives

A. Synopsis

Pat and Lee are college students and are co-workers in an office. They are both actively involved in Deaf club athletics and live in the same dormitory. Pat says s/he heard that something happened and asks Lee what's up. Lee asks if Pat remembers the trophy that s/he won at the basketball tournament last year. Pat asks if Lee means the American Athletic Association of the Deaf tournament in Houston. Lee nods and then says that someone stole the trophy. Pat asks how it happened. Lee replies that s/he doesn't know. Last night s/he was reading and the trophy was on the table and a cup was behind it. This morning the trophy was gone and the cup was tipped over. Pat asks if Lee's roommate borrowed the trophy. Lee says that's impossible because his/her roommate flew to Chicago last week. Pat asks if Lee feels it was someone walking by who noticed it and went in the room and stole it. Lee says it seems that's what happened.

B. Cultural Information: American Athletic Association of the Deaf

The American Athletic Association of the Deaf, Inc. (AAAD) is a national organization devoted to fostering and regulating athletic competition among member clubs. There are approximately 160 member clubs and approximately 20,000 individual members. There are seven regional divisions within the AAAD: Eastern Athletic Association of the Deaf (EAAD), Central Athletic Association of the Deaf (CAAD), Midwest Athletic Association of the Deaf (MAAD), Far West Athletic Association of the Deaf (FWAAD), Southwest Athletic Association of the Deaf (SWAAD), Southeastern Athletic Association of the Deaf (SEAAD), and Northwest Athletic Association of the Deaf (NWAAD).

The AAAD works to develop standard rules for inter-club competition and to provide adequate inter-club competition for its members. Toward this end, the AAAD sponsors an annual national basketball tournament and an annual softball tournament. The AAAD also gives an annual award to the Deaf Athlete of the Year and has a Hall of Fame which honors deaf (as well as hearing) players, leaders, and coaches. Finally, the AAAD participates in selecting and sponsoring deaf and hard-of-hearing athletes to participate in the Summer and Winter World Games for the Deaf. For further information about the AAAD, write: Secretary/Treasurer, American Athletic Association of the Deaf, 3916 Latern Drive, Silver Spring, Maryland 20902.

C. Dialogue

Pat

Pat₁: ‾‾‾‾co‾‾‾‾‾   ‾‾‾‾‾‾‾‾‾‾‾‾‾wh-q‾‾‾‾‾‾
        ME   HEAR+   (2h)WHAT'S-UP   (2h)"WHAT"
        "HEY"

Pat₂: ‾‾‾‾(nod‾‾‾‾‾‾)q‾‾‾‾
        THAT-ONE   INDEX-*rt*   A-A-A-D   HOUSTON   INDEX-*rt*   THAT-ONE

Pat₃: ‾‾‾‾‾‾‾‾‾‾wh-q‾‾‾‾‾‾
        "OH-MY",   "WHAT"   HOW   HAPPEN   HOWwg

Pat₄: ‾‾‾‾‾‾‾‾‾‾‾‾‾‾‾‾‾‾‾‾‾‾‾‾‾‾‾‾‾‾‾‾q‾‾‾‾‾
        ROOMMATE   BORROW-FROM-*you*

Pat₅: ‾‾‾‾(gaze lf   )‾‾‾‾   q
        YOU ‾‾‾‾FEEL   SOMEONE   1-CL-*rt*'person walk by'   NOTICE-TO-*lf*   GO-INTO-*lf*   SWIPE-*lf*
        YOU ‾‾‾‾‾‾‾‾‾‾‾→   *YOU*

Lee

Lee₁:
$\overline{\text{nodding}}$ <u>   q</u>
REMEMBER ONE-YEAR-PAST BASKETBALL TOURNAMENT,

<u>   q</u>
EXCITE WIN, (2h)*lf***-GIVE-TO-***me*** TROPHY, REMEMBER**

Lee₂: **SOMEONE STEAL**

Lee₃:
     <u>   neg   </u> <u>   t   </u>   <u>(gaze rt)</u> <u>nodding</u>
NOT-KNOW, PAST NIGHT, ME READ+, INDEX-*rt*** TABLE,**

          <u>(gaze rt)</u>
TROPHY A-CL@*rt*** ────────────────────────────────▶**
                    C-U-P   C-CL@rt,cntr 'cup behind trophy'

<u>   t   </u>
MORNING, SNATCHED-UP-*trophy*** C-CL-***rt*** } 'cup on table is turned on its side' "HUH"**
                              B↑-CL-***rt*** }

Lee₄:
<u>   neg   </u>
NOT-POSSIBLE, NOT HERE FROM-*here***-FLY-TO-***lf*** CHICAGO ONE-WEEK-PAST**

Lee₅:
<u>   neg   </u> <u>nodding</u>
NOT-KNOW SEEM+

D. Key Illustrations

Pat

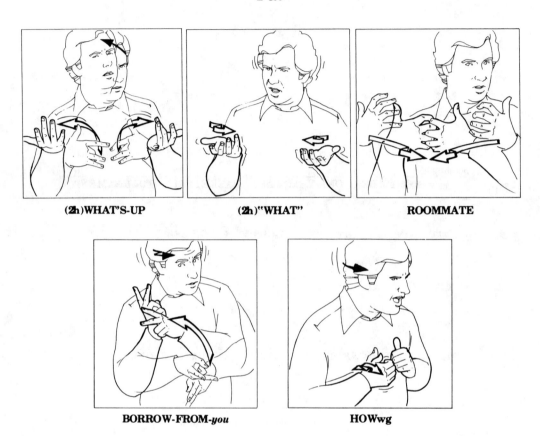

(2h)WHAT'S-UP   (2h)"WHAT"   ROOMMATE

BORROW-FROM-*you*   HOWwg

Lee

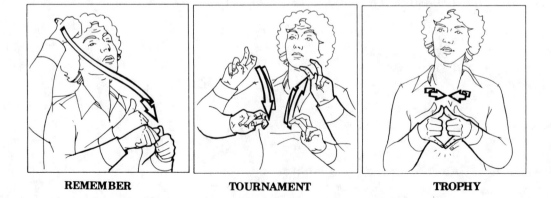

REMEMBER   TOURNAMENT   TROPHY

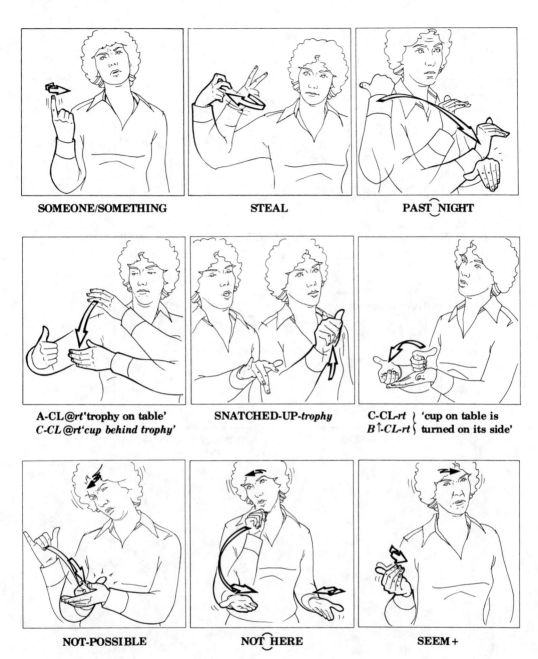

SOMEONE/SOMETHING   **STEAL**   **PAST NIGHT**

A-CL@*rt* 'trophy on table'   **SNATCHED-UP**-*trophy*   C-CL-*rt* } 'cup on table is
C-CL@*rt* 'cup behind trophy'   B↑-CL-*rt* } turned on its side'

NOT-POSSIBLE   **NOT HERE**   **SEEM +**

E. Supplementary Illustrations

THAT-ONE

NOTICE-TO-*rt*

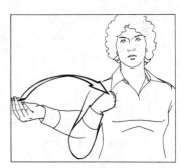

rt*-GIVE-TO-*me

NOT-KNOW

FROM-*here*-FLY-TO-*rt*

F. General Discussion: Locatives

Locatives are ways of describing the spatial relationship between two or more people, places, or things. In English, prepositional phrases are used to describe spatial relationships. For example, the prepositional phrases in the sentences 'The boy is *under the car*' and 'The girl is *in the room*' describe the spatial relationship between the 'boy' and the 'car' and between the 'girl' and the 'room'. The following diagram illustrates several different types of spatial relationships and how these are described with English prepositions.

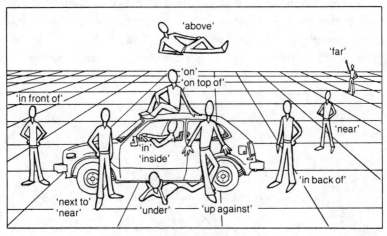

Fig. 6.1 Some spatial relationships

Unlike English, ASL generally does not use a separate sign (like a preposition) to describe a spatial relationship. Instead, ASL tends to use the signing space to illustrate how people, places, or things are spatially related. Very often this involves using a classifier in a specific location or using a directional verb to show where something happens. For example, to describe the location of a 'boy' in relation to a 'car', the Signer would probably use two classifiers: 3→CL 'car' and V ↓-CL 'person standing'. The 3→CL'car' would be made with one hand, and the V↓-CL'person standing' would be made with the other hand and positioned in the spatial relationship to the car that the Signer wants to describe. Figure 6.2 shows three possible relationships between the car and the person.

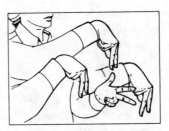

**Fig. 6.2   A person standing 'behind', 'above', and
'in front of' a car**

Notice that this way of indicating spatial relationships very often involves the use of both hands. One hand is often 'stationary' and the other is placed in a specific spatial relationship to the first hand. Because of this, ASL often gives more exact information about spatial relationships than English normally does. For example, suppose the Signer wants to describe the relationship between a car and a girl who is standing 'next to' the car. Where will the Signer position the 'V' handshape classifier? If the Signer puts it next to the 'car' fingers, then the girl is shown standing 'next to the front of' the car. If the Signer puts it next to the wrist of the other hand, then the girl is described as standing 'next to the back of' the car. Three possible locations of the 'person standing' classifier are illustrated in Figure 6.3.

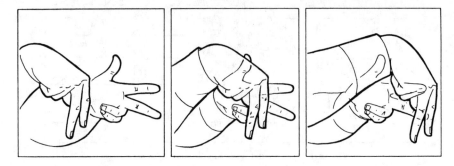

Fig. 6.3   Person standing next to different parts of a car

Similarly, in Unit 5, the 'car' classifiers showed exactly where one car smashed into the other—the left rear.

3→CL'car stopped'
3→CL'car from left smash into left rear'

If, in this example, the left hand **3→CL** had contacted ('hit') the fingertips of the right hand **3→CL**, the meaning would have been 'smash into left front'. Not only can ASL convey exact spatial information by using classifiers, but often it does so in a way that is much more efficient and concise than English.

Another way of indicating spatial relationships in ASL is by using directional verbs. These verbs can indicate the location of an action or event by moving the verb from one spatial location to another spatial location. Consider, for example, the verb **FROM-____-FLY-TO-____**. This verb indicates the place of origin and the place of destination by moving from one location to another. If the Signer has previously established the city 'Atlanta' to his/her right and then if the sign moves to the right, the meaning is 'from here fly to Atlanta'. However, if the sign moves from the right and toward the Signer, the meaning is 'from Atlanta fly to here'.

 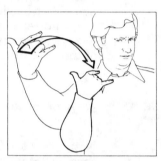

FROM-*here*-FLY-TO-*atlanta*   **FROM-*atlanta*-FLY-TO-*here***

Some signs can show exactly where an action occurs by making the sign at a specific location on the body. This is illustrated in Unit 4 with the sign **SHAVE-____**. Another sign which is similar is **HAVE-OPERATION-ON-____**.

HAVE-OPERATION-ON-*head*   **HAVE-OPERATION-ON-*heart***

HAVE-OPERATION-ON-*shoulder*

There are several other ways to describe locative relationships in ASL and these will be discussed in future units. In general, it is important to remember that ASL usually indicates locative relationships by using the signing space and not by using separate signs.

G. Text Analysis

Lee$_1$:

nodding ——— q
REMEMBER ONE-YEAR-PAST BASKETBALL TOURNAMENT,

q
EXCITE WIN, (2h)*lf*-GIVE-TO-*me* TROPHY, REMEMBER

- (2h)*lf*-**GIVE-TO**-*me*

  Notice that this is a sign which can indicate the subject and object by changing the direction of movement. (This type of directional verb is described in Unit 4.) Since no one has been given that location to the left, the meaning of the verb (using both hands) is like 'they give me'.

Pat$_2$:

(nod)q
THAT-ONE INDEX-*rt* A-A-A-D HOUSTON INDEX-*rt* THAT-ONE

Notice that the Signer uses the sign **INDEX**-*rt* to assign a specific location in the signing space to the A.A.A.D. tournament in Houston. For further information about how Signers 'set up' things in space, see Unit 3.

The sign **HOUSTON** is made by tapping the handshape used to represent the letter **'H'** on the side of the chin.

Notice also that the entire sentence is a question and that the Signer uses the non-manual behaviors for asking 'yes-no' questions which are described in Unit 1.

Lee$_3$:

neg t (gaze rt) nodding
NOT-KNOW, PAST⁀NIGHT, ME READ+, INDEX-*rt* TABLE,

(gaze rt)
TROPHY A-CL@*rt* ————————→
C-U-P C-CL @rt,cntr 'cup behind trophy'

t
MORNING, SNATCHED-UP-*trophy* C-CL-*rt* / *B↑-CL-rt* } 'cup on table is turned on its side' "HUH"

- neg
  NOT-KNOW

  Notice that this sign is accompanied by the non-manual behaviors used to express negation. A description of these behaviors can be found in Unit 1.

<pre>   (gaze rt   ) nodding</pre>
- **INDEX-*rt* TABLE,**

> Indexing (pointing) is often used in ASL to assign a per-
> son, place, or thing to a particular location in the signing
> space. In this case, it is clear that the table is located to
> the Signer's right. Sometimes the index will occur after
> the noun it refers to has been signed. See Unit 3 for more
> information about this use of indexing.
>
> Notice that the Signer also gazes to the right while
> signing **INDEX-*rt*.** This is an example of how a Signer's
> manual and non-manual behaviors 'agree with' each
> other.

<pre>   (gaze rt   )</pre>
- **TROPHY   A-CL@***rt* ⎯⎯⎯⎯⎯⎯⎯⎯⎯⎯⎯⎯⎯⎯⎯→
    C-U-P   C-CL @rt,cntr'cup behind trophy'

> Here the **A-CL** is used to represent the trophy. It is lo-
> cated to the right where the table is located, thus convey-
> ing the meaning 'on the table'. If the Signer wished to
> convey a meaning different than what you would nor-
> mally expect (e.g. the trophy is *under* the table), then s/he
> probably would use one hand to represent the table and
> the other to represent the exact location of the trophy
> (under, next to, etc.).
>
> Notice that the Signer holds the **A-CL@***rt* in order to
> indicate the exact spatial relationship between the cup
> and the trophy. The Signer fingerspells **C-U-P** with the
> left hand (since the right hand is 'busy') and then uses a
> classifier (**C-CL**) to represent the 'cup'. This enables the
> Signer to show the exact location of the cup (on the table)
> and its relation to the trophy (behind the trophy).

- **SNATCHED-UP-***trophy*

> This is an example of a sign that is made in a particular
> location and indicates what the object is. Here the sign is
> made in the same location in which the Signer has estab-
> lished the trophy. Thus, it is clear that the trophy, not the
> cup, was stolen. The Signer further clarifies this by ex-
> plaining what happened to the cup.

- **C-CL-***rt* ⎫
  B↑-CL-*rt* ⎬ 'cup on table turned on its side'

> Here the Signer again uses the **C-CL** to represent the cup.
> It is still clear that this classifier is being used to repre-
> sent a cup (rather than something else) because of the
> Signer's earlier comments. It is also clear that the clas-
> sifier **B↑-CL** represents the table top. By positioning the
> **C-CL** in a certain way on top of the **B↑-CL,** the Sign-
> er describes what happened to the cup —it was turned
> over on its side on top of the table.

Pat₄: <u>ROOMMATE   BORROW-FROM-*you*</u>   q

- **BORROW-FROM-*you***

    This is another verb which can indicate the subject and/or
    object by changing its direction of movement.

Lee₄: <u>NOT-POSSIBLE,   NOT HERE   FROM-*here*-FLY-TO-*lf*   CHICAGO   ONE-WEEK-PAST</u>   neg

- <u>**NOT-POSSIBLE   NOT HERE**</u>   neg

    Notice that both of these signs are accompanied by the
    non-manual behaviors used for negation. These behaviors
    are described in Unit 1.
    Notice also that the sign **NOT HERE** is an example of
    two signs which frequently occur together. Because of
    this, certain changes may take place which make them
    look like a single sign.

- **FROM-*here*-FLY-TO-*lf***

    This is an example of a directional verb which provides
    locative information by moving from one spatial location
    to another spatial location. See the *General Discussion*
    section for further explanation of verbs of this type.

Pat₅: (gaze lf)   q
<u>FEEL   SOMEONE   1-CL-*rt*'person walk by'   NOTICE-TO-*lf*   GO-INTO-*lf*   SWIPE-*lf*</u>
YOU ————————————→   *YOU*

- **1-CL-*rt*'person walking by'**

    This is an example of a classifier which is used as a verb
    and shows where something happens. Lee's room (with
    table, trophy, etc.) has been located to Lee's right and
    Pat's left. This classifier moves in a way which conveys
    the meaning 'walk past your room'.

- (gaze lf)
  NOTICE-TO-*lf*

    Here the Signer uses the verb **NOTICE-TO-____** which
    can indicate what was 'noticed' by moving toward some-
    thing that has previously been established in space. In
    this instance, the thing noticed is Lee's trophy since the
    spatial location of the trophy was used in producing the
    sign **NOTICE-TO-*lf*.**
    Notice also that the Signer gazes to the left while pro-
    ducing the sign.

- **GO-INTO-*lf***

    This sign provides locative information by moving toward
    a specific location in space. Here the sign is produced to
    Pat's left—indicating that someone went into Lee's room.

- **SWIPE-*lf***

> This sign can be produced with one or two hands. In this
> case, the left hand is open (palm down) and the right hand
> suddenly changes from an open hand to a closed fist un-
> derneath the left hand (as if taking something away from
> under the left hand). Notice that the sign is produced to
> Pat's left—again referring to the location previously
> given to the trophy.

H. Sample Drills

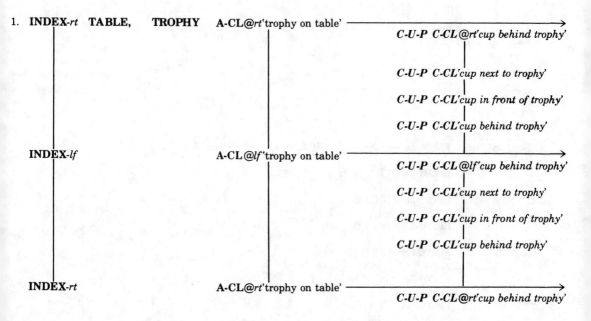

1. **INDEX-*rt* TABLE,   TROPHY**   **A-CL@*rt*'**trophy on table' ——————————————————————————→
   C-U-P C-CL@rt'cup behind trophy'

   C-U-P C-CL'cup next to trophy'

   C-U-P C-CL'cup in front of trophy'

   C-U-P C-CL'cup behind trophy'

   INDEX-*lf*   **A-CL@*lf*'**trophy on table' ——————————————————————————→
   C-U-P C-CL@lf'cup behind trophy'

   C-U-P C-CL'cup next to trophy'

   C-U-P C-CL'cup in front of trophy'

   C-U-P C-CL'cup behind trophy'

   INDEX-*rt*   **A-CL@*rt*'**trophy on table' ——————————————————————————→
   C-U-P C-CL@rt'cup behind trophy'

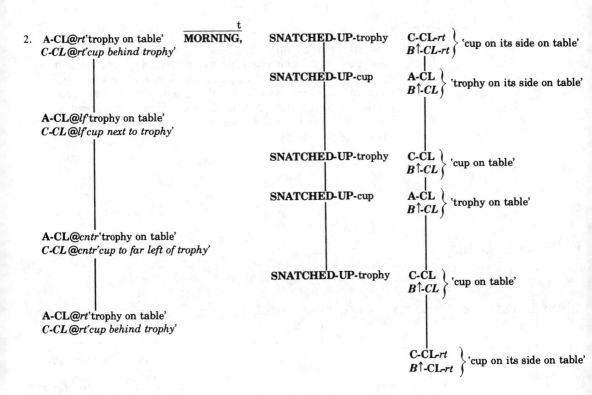

2. **A-CL@***rt*'trophy on table' $\overline{\text{MORNING,}}^{\text{t}}$ **SNATCHED-UP**-trophy   **C-CL-***rt* $\Big\}$ 'cup on its side on table'
   C-CL@*rt*'cup behind trophy'   **B↑-CL-***rt*

                                                            SNATCHED-UP-cup   **A-CL** $\Big\}$ 'trophy on its side on table'
                                                                                      B↑-CL

   A-CL@*lf*'trophy on table'
   C-CL@*lf*'cup next to trophy'

                                                            SNATCHED-UP-trophy   **C-CL** $\Big\}$ 'cup on table'
                                                                                      B↑-CL

                                                            SNATCHED-UP-cup   **A-CL** $\Big\}$ 'trophy on table'
                                                                                      B↑-CL

   A-CL@*cntr*'trophy on table'
   C-CL@*cntr*'cup to far left of trophy'

                                                            SNATCHED-UP-trophy   **C-CL** $\Big\}$ 'cup on table'
                                                                                      B↑-CL

   A-CL@*rt*'trophy on table'
   C-CL@*rt*'cup behind trophy'

                                                                                      C-CL-*rt* $\Big\}$ 'cup on its side on table'
                                                                                      B↑-CL-*rt*

3. $\overline{\text{NOT-POSSIBLE,}}^{\text{neg}}$ **FROM-***here*-**FLY-TO-***lf* **CHICAGO ONE-WEEK-PAST**

   FROM-*here*-**FLY-TO-***rt*

   FROM-*here*-**DRIVE-TO-***rt*

   FROM-*here*-**DRIVE-TO-***lf*

   FROM-*here*-**GO-TO-***lf*

   FROM-*here*-**GO-TO-***rt*

   FROM-*here*-**FLY-TO-***rt*

   FROM-*here*-**FLY-TO-***lf*

I. Video Notes

If you have access to the videotape package designed to accompany these texts, you will notice the following:

- The beginning of Lee's first turn is a question. However, Pat answers the question by nodding while Lee is signing. Thus, Lee does not have to wait for Pat's answer since it is already clear that Pat does remember the basketball tournament. Consequently, Lee continues to give more information after asking the question.

- Notice that when Lee says that he was reading last night (Lee₃), he uses a particular facial behavior which conveys the meaning 'normally' or 'regularly'.

- Notice that when Lee sets up the classifier **A-CL** to his right, he also gazes in that direction. This is an example of how a Signer's eye gaze will often 'agree with' the location of the thing that is being described.

- When Lee is describing how the cup was turned on its side on the table, he uses a particular facial behavior which conveys the meaning 'carelessly' or 'without paying attention'.

- Notice that Pat frequently nods or shakes her head while Lee is describing what happened to his trophy. This type of feedback is very helpful because it lets the Signer know that the other person understands.

Unit 7
Pluralization

A. Synopsis

Pat and Lee meet on a street corner. Pat knows that Lee has at least one school-aged child but asks Lee how many children she has. Lee replies that she has two—a seven year old girl and a three year old boy. Pat asks if the girl (who is deaf) goes to the residential school. Lee replies that she doesn't go there yet; right now she commutes to a hearing school. Pat asks if there are many deaf students there. Lee says there are a few deaf students but lots of hearing students. Pat asks if the teachers are any good. Lee says that they're "so-so". There are two teachers: one is sorta o.k.; the other has deaf parents and is a skilled Signer. Pat asks if Lee has gone to observe the class yet. Lee says that she hasn't but her husband has. He went into the room and it was strange—all the kids were lying on the floor sleeping so there was nothing to observe. After talking with the two teachers, he left.

B. Cultural Information: Mainstreaming

In 1975, the government passed a public law (Education for All Handicapped Children Act) which was designed to make sure all handicapped children are placed in appropriate educational programs. This public law (PL 94-142) has resulted in an increased number of "mainstreamed" or "integrated" programs. *Mainstreaming* is a term used to describe an educational situation in which a deaf child spends all or part of the school day in classes with hearing children. This includes programs in which a deaf student is integrated into a couple of classes with hearing children but spends most of his/her time in classes with other deaf students. There are also many special programs for deaf students in schools for hearing students. In these programs, the deaf students do not attend classes with hearing students but stay in what are called "special education classes".

According to a 1977 report from the Office of Demographic Studies (ODS) at Gallaudet College, approximately 20% of all deaf students are "mainstreamed". Another 22% of them are enrolled in full-time special education classes located within schools for hearing students.

Full implementation of PL 94-142 occurred on September 1, 1978. Under this law, each state is responsible for a free, "appropriate" education for all handicapped children. The way schools decide what is or is not "appropriate" is by using an Individualized Educational Program (IEP). The IEP is supposed to consider the child's present level of performance, determine the child's needs, and state goals which must be met during the upcoming school year. IEPs are prepared each year for each child and must be approved or amended by the parent or guardian. For more information, contact: Coordinator, PL 94-142 Program, Pre-College Programs, Gallaudet College, Washington, D.C. 20002.

C. Dialogue

Pat

Pat₁:
$$\overline{\quad\overset{co}{\text{"HEY"},}}\quad\text{CURIOUS,}\quad\overline{\text{CHILDREN}\quad\text{HOW-MANY}\quad\overset{wh\text{-}q}{\text{YOU}}}$$

Pat₂:
$$\text{OH-I-SEE,}\quad\overline{\text{GIRL}\quad\text{INDEX-}\textit{lf}\quad\overset{q}{\text{DEAF,}}}\quad\overline{\text{GO-TO-}\textit{rt}\quad\overset{q}{\text{STATE-SCHOOL}}}$$

Pat₃:
$$\overline{\text{MANY}\quad\text{DEAF}\quad\overset{q}{\text{INDEX-}\textit{lf}}}$$

Pat₄:
$$\overline{\text{TEACH⌒AGENT}\quad\text{GROUP}\quad\text{GOOD+}\quad\overset{q}{\text{INDEX-}\textit{lf}}}$$

Pat₅:
$$\overline{\text{FINISH}\quad\overset{(\text{gaze lf })}{\text{GO-TO-}\textit{lf}}\quad\overset{q}{\text{OBSERVE-}\textit{lf}}}$$

Lee

Lee₁:
          (body, gaze rt)   (body, gaze lf)   (body, gaze rt)   (body, gaze lf)
          GIRL-*rt*   **BOY**-*lf*   **AGE-SEVEN**-*rt* **AGE-THREE**-*lf*
   TWO,

Lee₂:
                neg
   NOT-YET, (2h)**NOW** **HEARING** **SCHOOL** **COMMUTE-BETWEEN**-*here*-**AND**-*rt* ↔

Lee₃:
   neg
   HEARING (2h)**5:**↓**CL**'hordes of children', **DEAF** **FEW** **SEVEN** **EIGHT** **THEREABOUTS**

Lee₄:
   neg   t
   "SO-SO" ‾‾**TEACH‿AGENT**‾‾ , **HAVE** **INDEX**-*lf index finger* **#OK** **"SO-SO"**,
                   TWO ————————————————————————→

   INDEX-*lf middle finger* **MOTHER‿FATHER** **DEAF,** **SKILL*** **SIGN**
   ————————————————————————————→

Lee₅:
   neg   nodding (gaze rt)   ‾‾t (gaze rt   )
   ME **NOT-YET,** **HUSBAND** **GO-TO**-*rt* **ROOM,** **GO-INTO**-*room,*

                (gaze down   )
   STRANGE, **FLOOR** **KID** (2h)**alt.V-CL**'kids lying on floor' **SLEEP,**

                                                          t
   OBSERVE (2h)**NOTHING*,** **HUSBAND** **TEACH‿AGENT** **THOSE-THREE**-*cntr,*

             br.raise
   TALK++-*arc* **FINISH,** **LEAVE-TO**-*rt*

D. Key Illustrations

Pat

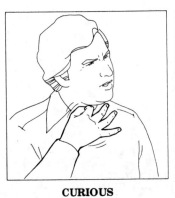

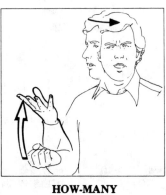

CURIOUS   **HOW-MANY**   **OBSERVE-***lf*

Lee

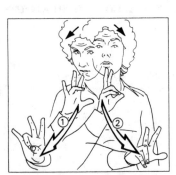

AGE-SEVEN-*rt* **AGE-THREE-***lf*   **NOT-YET**   **COMMUTE-BETWEEN-***here*-**AND-***rt* ↔

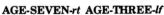

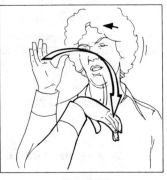

SKILL*   **HUSBAND**   **STRANGE**

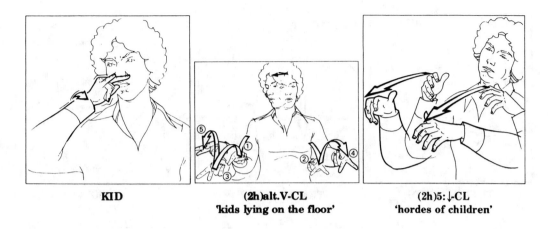

KID

(2h)alt.V-CL
'kids lying on the floor'

(2h)5:↓-CL
'hordes of children'

E. Supplementary Illustrations

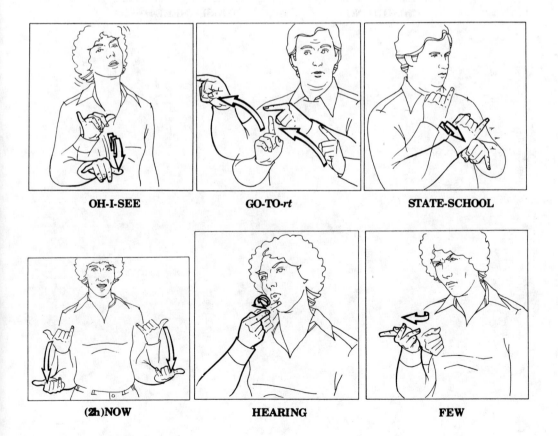

OH-I-SEE

GO-TO-*rt*

STATE-SCHOOL

(2h)NOW

HEARING

FEW

THEREABOUTS

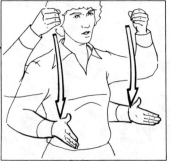

TEACH AGENT

"SO-SO"

(2h)NOTHING*

THOSE-THREE-*rt*

F. General Discussion: Pluralization

The term *pluralization* refers to the process or processes that are used in a language to indicate that there is more than one of something. For example, English speakers can indicate that there is more than one 'book' by adding an 's' to make the plural 'books'. English also uses words like 'a *row* of books', 'a *stack* of books', 'a *pile* of books', or '*lots* of books' to show that there is more than one book. There are several ways to show that something is plural in ASL. This discussion will focus on some of them.

Classifiers like **3→CL, A-CL,** and **C-CL** are *singular*—they represent one thing. To indicate more than one thing, these classifiers must be repeated. When the classifier is produced twice, it indicates that there are two things. If the classifier is made three times, it either means 'three' things or 'some' things. If it is produced more slowly (as if actually representing the location of each thing), then the meaning is 'three' things. If the classifier is made three (or four) times but is made faster and with less attention to the actual location of each thing, then the meaning is 'some'. If the Signer wants to focus on the exact number, s/he can use a particular number sign (e.g. **THREE**) and then sign the repeated classifier.

For example, if a Signer wants to indicate that there are 'five pencils in a row', s/he might sign **PENCIL FIVE** and then use the following classifier:

1→CL"*in a row*"(pencils)

Notice that the **1→CL** does not have to be repeated *five* times, but it must indicate that the noun (**PENCIL**) is plural (which it does by repetition). Although the specific number of pencils—five—has already been shown with the sign **FIVE**, the classifier must be repeated to 'agree with' the fact that the number of pencils is plural. Notice also that the classifier gives information about the spatial relationship of the pencils to each other—they are next to each other. If the pencils are just scattered all over, then the classifier will be repeated in a different way, as shown in the illustration below. Again, there are not five repetitions of the **1→CL**, but simply enough to indicate plurality. (However, the number of repetitions cannot be greater than the actual numbers of things. For example, the sign illustrated below cannot be used to describe 'three' pencils).

(2h)alt.1→CL'pencils scattered'

Notice that in this illustration the Signer uses two hands—a **1→CL** on each hand. This "two hands alternating" movement is often used to indicate that there are a plural number of things or people positioned in an unorderly or disorganized fashion. For example, if the Signer wishes to indicate that there are many papers scattered all over a desk, then s/he might use a **B↓-CL** to represent each paper and the '(2h)alt.' movement to show that there are several of them scattered on top of the desk.

(2h)alt.B↓-CL'papers scattered'

As we saw in the first illustration of 'pencils in a row', classifiers can be used to show that there are some, several, or many things in a row. To do this, the Signer repeats the classifier with the dominant hand while the non-dominant hand 'holds' the start of the row. Thus, if the Signer wants to indicate that there are several trophies in a row, s/he will probably use the **A-CL** to represent each trophy and then show that there are several of them in a row by signing:

(2h)A-CL"*in a row*"(trophies)

If there is more than one row of trophies, then the Signer will repeat the 'row' and sign each added row in a different location.

(2h)A-CL*"in rows"*(trophies)

Some classifiers are already *plural*. Classifier handshapes like the one illustrated below on the left refer to a specific number. We saw this in the illustration of *'two come up to me'* in Unit 6. Other classifier handshapes like the one illustrated below on the right refer to a larger, unspecified number. Thus, these classifiers will also indicate that the noun is plural.

Another obvious way to indicate that the noun is plural is to use a specific number sign (**TWO, FIVE,** etc.) or a non-specific number sign (**MANY, FEW,** etc.). In general, the specific number sign will occur before the noun. However, some Signers (especially older Signers) tend to sign the number after the noun. If the number has special significance, then it is often signed after the noun and is stressed. This draws attention to the number. If a number sign and a classifier are used to refer to the same noun in a sentence, then generally the number sign will come after the noun and the classifier will be last—e.g. **TROPHY FOUR A-CL***"in a row"*.

Another way to indicate that the noun is plural is to repeat the noun itself. However, this is only possible with a limited number of nouns (**HOUSE, STREET, STATUE,** etc.). And if a number sign is used (e.g. **TWO HOUSE**), then the noun usually is *not* repeated—unless the Signer wants to establish spatial locations for each thing for later use.

These are some of the ways that ASL Signers indicate that a noun is plural. Other ways to do this will be discussed in later units.

G. Text Analysis

$$\overline{\quad\text{co}\quad}$$
$$\overline{\qquad\qquad\qquad\qquad\text{wh-q}\qquad\qquad}$$
Pat$_1$:   **"HEY"**,   **CURIOUS**,   **CHILDREN HOW-MANY YOU**

- **CHILDREN**

  This is an example of how a noun (**CHILD/SMALL**) can be made plural by repetition. This sign can be made with one or two hands.

	(body, gaze rt)	(body, gaze lf)	(body, gaze rt)	(body, gaze lf)
Lee$_1$:	**GIRL**-*rt*	**BOY**-*lf*	**AGE-SEVEN**-*rt*	**AGE-THREE**-*lf*
TWO,				

(body,gaze rt   )   (body,gaze lf   )
- **AGE-SEVEN**-*rt*   **AGE-THREE**-*lf*

  Notice that the Signer produces the sign **AGE-SEVEN** in the same general location that was assigned to the 'girl' (to the right) and the sign **AGE-THREE** in the same general location as was given to the 'boy' (to the left).

  Notice also that since the signs **GIRL** and **BOY** cannot be easily moved in space, the Signer's body tilts slightly to the right and left to help give them particular locations. Since the Signer also tilts to the right when signing **AGE-SEVEN** and to the left when signing **AGE-THREE**, it is clear that the girl is seven years old and the boy is three years old.

$$\overline{\qquad\qquad\qquad\qquad\qquad\text{q}\qquad\qquad}\quad\overline{\qquad\text{q}\qquad}$$
Pat$_2$:   **OH-I-SEE**,   **GIRL   INDEX**-*lf*   **DEAF**,   **GO-TO**-*rt*   **STATE-SCHOOL**

$$\overline{\qquad\qquad\qquad\qquad\text{q}\qquad}$$
- **GIRL   INDEX**-*lf*   **DEAF**,

  Notice that the Signer refers to the girl by pointing to the left. This is the same location in which Lee signed **GIRL** and **AGE-SEVEN**.

  Notice also that Pat is asking Lee a 'yes-no' question. Since Lee responds by nodding 'yes', Pat continues to ask another question. However, the non-manual behaviors used for asking yes-no questions are not 'dropped' after the first question. Rather, they are held and then continue on during the second question.

$$\overline{\quad\text{neg}\quad}$$
Lee$_2$:   **NOT-YET**,   (2h)**NOW   HEARING   SCHOOL   COMMUTE-BETWEEN**-*here*-**AND**-*rt* ↔

$$\overline{\quad\text{neg}\quad}$$
- **NOT-YET**

  Notice the non-manual behaviors used to indicate negation. For a description of these behaviors, see Unit 1.

- **COMMUTE-BETWEEN-*here*-AND-*rt*↔**

    This sign conveys the meaning of regular movement be-
    tween two locations. Even though the Signer does not
    sign **SCHOOL-*rt*,** the school is clearly given a location to
    Lee's right because the sign **COMMUTE-BETWEEN-
    ____-AND-____** moves back and forth between the Signer
    ('here') and the Signer's right ('the school').

    The double-headed arrow (↔) is a symbol which indi-
    cates that the sign moves back and forth between the two
    locations ('here' and 'right').

Pat₃:
$$\overline{\hspace{4.5cm}}^{\text{q}}$$
MANY   DEAF   INDEX-*lf*

- **INDEX-*lf***

    Notice that Pat points to the left to refer to the hearing
    school. This is the location that Lee has just established
    with the sign **COMMUTE-BETWEEN-*here*-AND-*rt*↔.**

Lee₃:
$$\overline{\hspace{1.5cm}}^{\text{neg}}$$
HEARING   (2h)5:↓CL'hordes of children',   **DEAF   FEW   SEVEN   EIGHT   THEREABOUTS**

- **(2h)5: ↓-CL 'hordes of children'**

    This classifier (which can be made with one or two hands)
    is an example of a classifier which is already plural. It has
    the general meaning 'too many to count'. In this case, it
    refers to the number of hearing students at the school.

- **FEW**

    This is an example of a non-specific number sign. The
    signs **SEVERAL** and **FEW** are similar except that the
    sign **SEVERAL** has a larger movement and has more
    fingers extended. In addition, different non-manual be-
    haviors usually occur with these signs. Compare the illus-
    tration of **FEW** (given above) with the two illustrations
    below. Also notice how the sign on the right indicates a
    larger number of things than the sign on the left.

SEVERAL   **SEVERAL**

- **SEVEN   EIGHT   THEREABOUTS**

  This is an example of two specific number signs (**SEVEN   EIGHT**). However, since the Signer is not sure exactly how many Deaf students there are, the sign **THEREABOUTS** is used to indicate that **SEVEN EIGHT** is a "ballpark" figure.

$$\text{Pat}_4:$$
$$\overline{\text{TEACH⌢AGENT   GROUP   GOOD}+ \quad \text{INDEX-}lf}^{\quad\text{q}}$$

- **TEACH⌢AGENT   GROUP**

  The sign **GROUP** is actually a classifier (two hands C-CL) which shows that the noun **TEACH⌢AGENT** is plural.

- **INDEX-***lf*

  The direction of the point is to Pat's left (Lee's right) because this is the location that Lee 'assigned' to the hearing school with the sign **COMMUTE-BETWEEN-***here***-AND-***rt*↔.

$$\text{Lee}_4:$$

$$\overset{\text{neg}}{\text{"SO-SO"}} \quad \overset{\qquad\qquad\qquad\qquad\text{t}}{\text{TEACH⌢AGENT}},\quad \text{HAVE}\quad \text{INDEX-}lf\,index\,finger\quad \#\text{OK}\quad \text{"SO-SO"},$$
TWO ⟶

INDEX-*lf middle finger* **MOTHER⌢FATHER   DEAF,   SKILL*   SIGN** ⟶

- **TEACH⌢AGENT** $\overset{\text{t}}{,}$
  TWO

  This is an example of a specific number sign used to indicate exactly how many teachers there are. Notice that the sign **TWO** is made with the left hand. This is because the Signer will refer to those two fingers on the left hand when describing each teacher.

- *TWO* **HAVE   INDEX-***lf index finger***   #OK   "SO-SO",** ⟶

  INDEX-*lf middle finger* **MOTHER⌢FATHER   DEAF,** ⟶

  This is an example of one way that Signers use the non-dominant hand when listing and describing two or more things. The Signer has indicated exactly how many teachers there are (two) and then proceeds to discuss each one. The first teacher is 'assigned' to the left index finger. If, later in the conversation, the Signer wants to make further comments about that teacher, then s/he will again use the left index finger to refer to that teacher. The second teacher is 'assigned' to the left middle finger.

Lee₅: $\overline{\text{neg}}$ $\overline{\text{nodding}}$ (gaze rt) $\overline{\text{t}}$ (gaze rt   )
       ME   NOT-YET,   HUSBAND   GO-TO-*rt* **ROOM,   GO-INTO**-*room,*

                   (gaze down   )
       STRANGE,   FLOOR   KID   (2h)alt.**V-CL**'kids lying on floor'   **SLEEP,**

                                                                          $\overline{\text{t}}$
       OBSERVE   (2h)**NOTHING*,   HUSBAND   TEACH AGENT   THOSE-THREE**-*cntr,*

                 $\overline{\text{br.raise}}$
       TALK++-*arc*   **FINISH,   LEAVE-TO**-*rt*

$\overline{\text{nodding}}$
- **HUSBAND**

    Like many other signs in ASL (e.g. **BROTHER,
    SISTER**), this sign was originally two separate signs
    (**MAN** and **MARRY**) that were made together to express
    the meaning 'husband'. Through time, the form of these
    two joined signs has changed, and they now have become
    one sign: **HUSBAND.** Notice that by nodding while pro-
    ducing this sign, the Signer indicates that her husband
    has already gone to observe in the school.

- **GO-INTO**-*room*

    This is an example of a verb which shows where the ac-
    tion occurred by being produced in a certain location. For
    further information, see Unit 6.

(gaze down   )
- **FLOOR   KID**   (2h)alt.**V-CL**'kids lying on floor'   **SLEEP**

    Notice that the classifier (**V-CL**) is produced with both
    hands (2h) and that the hands alternate (alt.). This indi-
    cates that the noun (**KID**) is plural and that the 'kids' are
    arranged in a *disorderly* (random) manner on the floor.
      Notice also how the Signer looks down while signing
    FLOOR and describing the kids on the floor.

- **OBSERVE**   (2h)**NOTHING***

    Notice that the sign **NOTHING** is made here with two
    hands. It can also be produced with one hand. Notice also
    that it is stressed (*). Here this means that the Signer
    holds the beginning of the sign longer than usual and that
    the movement of the sign is more tense than usual.

- **THOSE-THREE-***cntr*

  Here the Signer uses a pronoun which not only indicates the specific number of people involved (three), but also can be used to assign this group of three to a particular location (e.g. the center, the left, the right). This sign can also include the Signer in the group of three if it is made closer to the Signer's body. It then has the meaning 'the three of us'.

US-THREE

  If there are four people in a conversation, the Signer can express the meaning 'the three of you' by producing the sign in the general direction of the other three people:

YOU-THREE

  Many Signers also use the number **FOUR** and **FIVE** to express meanings like 'the five of us', 'the four of you', or 'the five of them'.

- **TALK++-***arc*

  The way this sign is made shows that the action involved several people. (In this case, three people talked with each other.) Adding an arc to a verb is a common way to indicate plurality. For example, if a Signer wishes to indicate that s/he met many people, then the sign **MEET** would probably be produced with an arc.

MEET+++-*arc*

H. Sample Drills

1. **HEARING** (2h)**5:↓-CL**'hordes of children', **DEAF FEW**

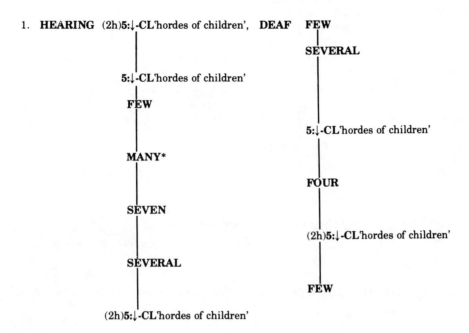

2. **FLOOR**

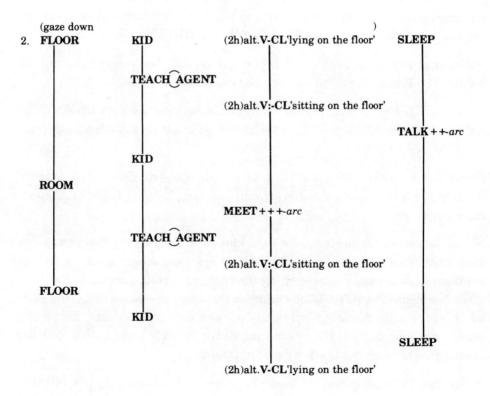

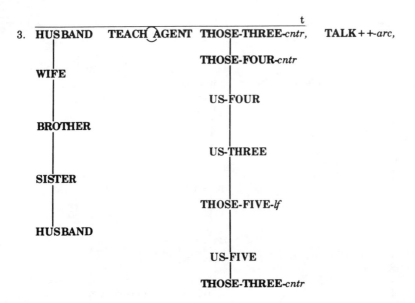

```
                                                    t
3.  HUSBAND     TEACH AGENT   THOSE-THREE-cntr,    TALK++-arc,

                             THOSE-FOUR-cntr
    WIFE

                             US-FOUR

    BROTHER

                             US-THREE

    SISTER

                             THOSE-FIVE-lf

    HUSBAND

                             US-FIVE

                         THOSE-THREE-cntr
```

I. Video Notes

If you have access to the videotape package designed to accompany these texts, you will notice the following:

- Notice how Lee leans slightly to the right and to the left in the first turn to give separate spatial locations to the 'girl' and the 'boy'. Notice that these locations are also used with the signs **AGE-SEVEN** and **AGE-THREE**.

- Notice that when Pat asks whether the girl is deaf, Lee responds simply by nodding. So Pat continues to ask another question.

- Notice that Lee uses a particular facial behavior with the sign **COMMUTE-BETWEEN**-*here*-**AND**-*rt*↔. This facial behavior conveys the meaning 'normally' or 'regularly'.

- Notice the facial behavior that Lee uses with the sign (2h)**5:**↓**CL**'hordes of children'. This facial behavior conveys the meaning 'awfully large' or 'surprisingly huge'.

- Notice that when Lee describes how the kids were lying on the floor, she gazes downward. This is a good example of how eye gaze often 'agrees with' the location of the person, place, or thing the Signer is talking about. Notice that when Lee signs (2h)alt.**V-CL**'kids lying on the floor', she uses a facial behavior which conveys the meaning 'carelessly' or 'not paying attention'. This facial behavior reinforces what the alternating hands indicate—the kids were lying around in a random or disorderly arrangement.

- Notice that Pat's portion of the dialogue consists almost entirely of questions. The 'one-shot' view of Pat provides several clear examples of the non-manual behaviors for asking 'yes-no' questions and 'wh-word' questions.

Unit 8

Temporal Aspect

A. Synopsis

Pat and Lee are good friends but haven't kept in touch for awhile. They meet on a street corner. Pat says that s/he hasn't seen Lee for some time, and asks what s/he's been doing. Lee says that s/he is still working at the residential school. Pat asks Lee exactly what his/her job is at the school. Lee is a dorm counselor and says that sometimes it's really boring! Every day there are meetings continually. Pat asks what the meetings are for. Lee explains that if a kid has a problem or there's some trouble, then in the afternoon, Lee and the teacher frequently discuss the situation with each other. Lee goes on to explain that after the discussion is over, s/he has to write a report. Lee is fed up with meetings every day and then having to write up reports. Pat asks why Lee doesn't quit. Lee has applied for another job and has sent in an application, but has waited for a long time and hasn't heard a thing.

B. Cultural Information: Deaf Dorm Counselors and Houseparents

In each residential school for Deaf students, there is a group of adults who deal with the students "after hours", when the students are not attending classes. Various titles have been given to these adults, including "houseparents", "dorm supervisors", and "dorm counselors". In many cases, these dorm counselors are required to live at the school. Quite often, such positions are advertised at relatively low salaries because room and board are included.

In the past, a large number of dorm counselors were Deaf and many of them worked at the same school they graduated from. For many students, these dorm counselors were their first sustained contact with Deaf adults. Thus, for these students, the dorm counselors often functioned as adult Deaf role models, disciplinarians, "alter" parents, tutors, and language models. As language models, these adults often helped the students learn ASL. Many Deaf people who attended residential programs recall one or more Deaf dorm supervisors who would tell stories or explain the day's lessons in a way that the students could understand and enjoy.

For some Deaf houseparents, the job was simply 'something to do' while they waited for a better opportunity to come along—like a teaching position or job outside the field of education. For others, the school became their home. They worked as dorm supervisors during the school year (and often as coaches or sponsors of various school organizations) and during the summer, they worked on the grounds or maintenance crews.

Now, however, the number of Deaf houseparents is decreasing. Housing problems, pay scales, and limited summer employment are some of the reasons why there are fewer and fewer Deaf dorm counselors. In addition, more jobs and better jobs are now being made available to Deaf people, so there is less incentive to accept and remain in the position of dorm counselor.

C. Dialogue

Pat

Pat₁:
$$\overline{\text{co}}$$ UP-TILL-NOW*   SEE-*you* NONE, $\overline{\text{(2h)}\textbf{WHAT'S-UP}}^{\text{wh-q}}$
"HEY"

Pat₂: $\overline{\text{YOUR   \#JOB   EXACT   (2h)}\textbf{"WHAT"}}^{\text{wh-q}}$

Pat₃: $\overline{\text{MEETING   FOR-FOR}}^{\text{wh-q}}$
                      "WHAT"

Pat₄: *OH-I-SEE*

Pat₅: $\overline{\text{WHY͡NOT   QUIT}}^{\text{wh-q}}$
                  "WHAT"

Pat₆: $\overline{\textit{HEAR͡NONE,}}^{\text{br.raise}}$ *OH-I-SEE*

Lee

ee₁: "WELL", STILL WORK INDEX-*lf* STATE-SCHOOL

           <u>nodding</u>
ee₂: ME <u>COUNSEL</u> INDEX-*lf* D-O-R-M, "UMMM" TRUE SOMETIMES BORED*,

EVERY-DAY MEETING*"over time"*

ee₃: "WELL", SUPPOSE KID PROBLEM, "WELL", TROUBLE SOMETHING,

                                 <u>(gaze lf)t</u>
"UH" AFTERNOON, TEACH AGENT   US-TWO-*lf*,

DISCUSS-WITH*"each other"* +*"regularly"*

                                <u>brow raise</u>   <u>t</u>
e₄: "UH" DISCUSS-WITH*"each other"* FINISH, <u>ME</u>+, WRITE, "PSHAW",

EVERY-DAY MEETING*"long time"*, "AND-THEN-WHAT" WRITE*"long time"*, "PSHAW" FED-UP*

                              <u>nodding</u>   <u>brow raise</u>
e₅: FINISH APPLY OTHER #JOB ME, <u>ME</u>+ *me*-SEND-TO-*lf*, ME WAIT*"long time"*

     <u>t</u>
UP-TILL-NOW, HEAR NONE INDEX-*lf*

D. Key Illustrations

Pat

SEE-*you* NONE   (2h)WHAT'S-UP   (2h)"WHAT"

MEETING   WHY NOT   QUIT

Lee

BORED*   MEETING"*over time*"   SUPPOSE

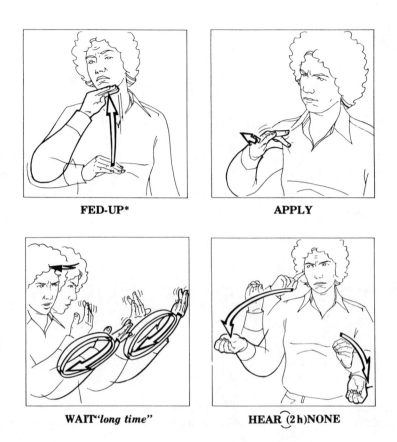

FED-UP*   APPLY

WAIT*"long time"*   HEAR (2h)NONE

E. Supplementary Illustrations

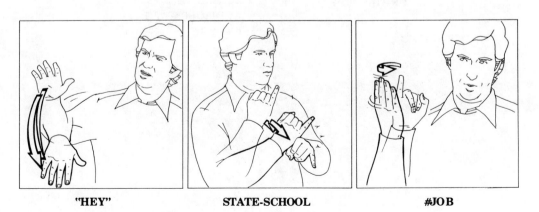

"HEY"   STATE-SCHOOL   #JOB

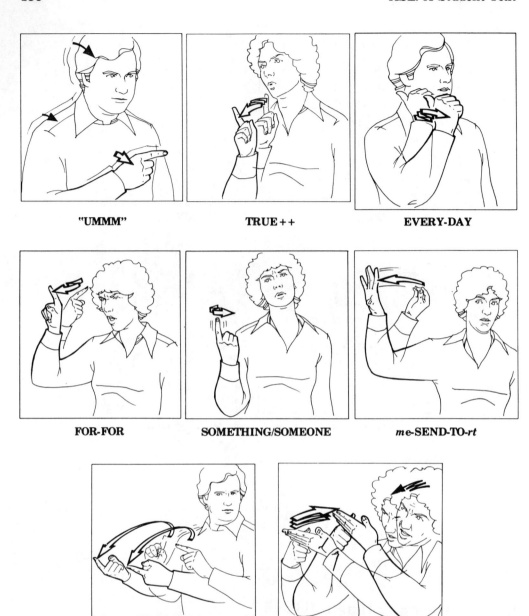

"UMMM"   TRUE++   EVERY-DAY

FOR-FOR   SOMETHING/SOMEONE   *m*e-SEND-TO-*rt*

UP-TILL-NOW

DISCUSS-WITH
"each other" +*"regularly"*

F. General Discussion: Temporal Aspect

The term *temporal aspect* refers to certain repeated movements that often occur with verbs in ASL to indicate things like how long an action lasts or how often the action occurs. These movements don't tell you specifically how long (e.g. 'two weeks') or how often (e.g. 'three times') the action occurs. Their meaning is more general — like 'for a long time' or 'regularly'.

For example, one of these movements is slow and elliptical, as illustrated below.

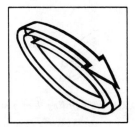

When this movement (modulation) is added to a verb, it means that something happened 'for a long time'. So we call this movement *"long time"*.

For example, suppose the Signer's sister fell and hurt herself and then cried for an hour. When describing what happened, the Signer might use the *"long time"* movement with the sign **CRY**, as illustrated below.

CRY*"long time"*

Or, suppose the Signer is fascinated by an unusual painting on the wall and has been staring at it for hours. That seems like a long time to be looking at something. This action ('looking at the painting') might then be described with the movement *"long time"*.

*me-**LOOK-AT**-painting"long time"*

Similarly, suppose the Signer has a hard time concentrating on things, so s/he rarely works for long periods of time. Then one day the Signer becomes really involved in a project and works on it for two straight hours. For the Signer, that feels like a very long time. S/he might describe her experience with the sign illustrated below.

WORK"long time"

An important thing to understand about this movement (and others like it) is that it indicates how the Signer feels about the length of time, but not how long that period actually is. For example, working for two hours may not feel like a long time for someone who works eight hours straight every day. That person would not use the *"long time"* movement to describe two hours of work. But for the Signer in the example above, that *is* a long time, and s/he would use the *"long time"* movement to describe what s/he did.

Another movement that can be added to a verb to indicate something about 'time' is illustrated below.

This small and straight-line repeated movement means that something happens 'repeatedly', 'frequently', 'a lot', or 'regularly'. So we call this movement *"regularly"*.

For example, suppose the Signer is walking with a friend and sees one of his/her favorite restaurants. The Signer might tell the friend "Oh, I go there often" or "I go there regularly". This would be signed as:

me-GO-TO-restaurant"regularly"

Or, suppose the unusual painting that was mentioned earlier is hanging on the wall in an office. One of the secretaries in the office keeps trying to figure out what the painting is supposed to be, so s/he looks at it frequently.

me-LOOK-AT-painting"regularly"

Notice how the movement of the verb _____ -**LOOK-AT-** _____ in the illustration above differs from the movement of the same verb with the *"long time"* movement. (See previous illustration.)

These kinds of temporal (time-related) movements can occur with many verbs in ASL (although not all of them). Notice that they can occur with directional verbs (See Unit 4)—where the movement of the verb also shows the subject and object. For example, the verb _____ -**LOOK-AT-** _____ can move from the person the Signer is talking with ('you') toward the Signer ('me') and can also show that the Signer feels that action is lasting for a 'long time': *you-***LOOK-AT**-*me"long time"*. Similarly, if the Signer's brother (located to the right) is really bothersome and regularly tries to interrupt what the Signer is doing, this might be expressed with the verb *brother-***BOTHER**-*me"regularly"*.

*brother-***BOTHER**-*me"regularly"*

Thus, you can see how different movements can communicate several different meanings in ASL.

This discussion has focused on two time-related modulations of signs: *"long time"* and *"regularly"*. Other similar types of movements will be discussed as they occur in later units.

G. Text Analysis

Pat₁:

        co   wh-q

              _____   UP-TILL-NOW*   SEE-*you* NONE,   _____

              "HEY"   (2h)**WHAT'S-UP**

- **UP-TILL-NOW***

    Notice that this is a stressed form of the sign. This means that the first part of the sign was made with a slow, tense movement. This adds the meaning that it's been a 'long time' since Pat saw Lee.

- **SEE-*you* NONE**

    This is another example of two signs which are frequently used together and which look like a single sign. Notice how these two signs seem to 'flow together'.

wh-q

Pat₂: _____

         YOUR   #JOB   EXACT   (2h)"WHAT"

- **#JOB**

    This is a fingerspelled loan sign in ASL. As with all fingerspelled loan signs, certain changes occur (generally dropping out the middle letter(s) and sometimes adding a particular movement) in the fingerspelled word to make it more like a regular ASL sign. Look at the illustration and notice that the middle letter—'O'—is not signed and that the palm faces the Signer on the 'B', following the natural flow of movement from the 'J'.

- **(2h)"WHAT"**

    This is a commonly-used, questioning gesture in ASL. This gesture can be made with either one or two hands.

Lee₂:
      <u>nodding</u>

ME   COUNSEL   INDEX-*lf*   D-O-R-M,   "UMMM"   TRUE   SOMETIMES   BORED*,

EVERY-DAY   MEETING*"over time"*

- **INDEX-*lf***

  Here the Signer points to the location previously 'assigned' to the state school (Lee₁) to indicate that the dorm is at the state school.

- **BORED***

  This is an example of a sign which has been stressed. Compare the illustration below with the illustration of the sign given above and note the differences. Which one seems more stressed?

BORED

- **EVERY-DAY**

  This sign is used not only to convey the meaning 'daily' or 'every day', but it is sometimes used to convey the meaning 'frequently'. Thus, in this sentence, the Signer may not actually mean that s/he has meetings every single day, but has them often enough so that it seems like every day.

- **MEETING*"over time"***

  This is an example of another movement often used with verbs to indicate that an action occurs 'for awhile' or 'continually'. This movement is small, repeated, and circular.

Pat$_3$: _____ wh-q

         MEETING   FOR-FOR
                              "WHAT"

- **FOR-FOR**

    This sign is used often in ASL when the Signer wants to
    know the reason or purpose for something. As such, it is a
    'wh-word' question sign like **WHY**. Notice that the non-
    manual behaviors used for 'wh-word' questions occur dur-
    ing the entire sentence.

- *"WHAT"*

    Notice that this sign is made only with the left hand and
    not with both hands as it was above (Pat$_2$).

Lee$_3$: **"WELL", SUPPOSE KID PROBLEM, "WELL", TROUBLE SOMETHING,**

                                              (gaze lf)t
         _____
         "UH" AFTERNOON, TEACH AGENT   US-TWO-*lf,*

         DISCUSS-WITH*"each other"* + *"regularly"*

- **SUPPOSE   KID   PROBLEM   "WELL",   TROUBLE   SOMETHING,**

    This is an example of what is called a *condition* in a condi-
    tional sentence. In general, conditional sentences have
    two parts—the condition (If . . .) and the result or conse-
    quence (. . . then . . .). Generally, in ASL, the condition is
    stated before the result. The condition (the "If . . . " por-
    tion) can be signaled by using the sign **SUPPOSE** (illus-
    trated above), by using the loan signs **#IF** or **#IFwg** (il-
    lustrated below), or solely through the use of specific
    non-manual behaviors.

#IF

#IFwg

- **AFTERNOON**

    There are at least two different forms of the sign **AFTERNOON.** One involves movement of the dominant hand and the other involves movement of the non-dominant hand.

AFTERNOON
(Variant A)

AFTERNOON
(Variant B)

- **US-TWO-***lf*

    This is an example of a plural pronoun. Notice that the exact number (two) is indicated with this pronoun (see Unit 3 for further information). Notice also that the pronoun is produced toward the left—the location previously given to the school where the meetings and discussions with the teacher take place.

- **DISCUSS-WITH***"each other"+"regularly"*

    This is an example of a verb in which two people together are acting as the subjects of the action (discussing). This is shown by moving the sign back and forth between the teacher and the Signer. The phrase *"each other"* is written after the verb to show that it has two subjects.

    This sign also illustrates one of the special verb movements discussed above—*"regularly"*. The meaning conveyed is that there are frequent or repeated discussions between the Signer and the teacher. Thus, the movement of this verb indicates how often the action occurs and also indicates that both the teacher and Lee are the subjects of the action.

<u>   brow raise   t   </u>

e₄: "UH" DISCUSS-WITH"*each other*" FINISH, ME+, WRITE, "PSHAW",

EVERY-DAY MEETING"*long time*", "AND-THEN-WHAT" WRITE"*long time*", "PSHAW" FED-UP*

- **MEETING**"*long time*"

  This is an example of one of the special verb movements discussed above—"*long time*". This movement is repeated and elliptical, and indicates that from the Signer's perspective, the action occurs for a prolonged period of time.

- **WRITE**"*long time*"

  This is another example of the "*long time*" movement. Notice that for the Signer, both the actions of 'meeting' and 'writing' are perceived as taking a long time.

- **FED-UP***

  Notice that the sign is stressed. In this case, the stressed form of this sign involves a stronger contact (of the back of the hand and the chin) than normal. The head also jerks back slightly when the contact is made.

<u>   nodding   brow raise   </u>

e₅: FINISH APPLY OTHER #JOB ME, ME+ *me*-SEND-TO-*lf*, ME WAIT"*long time*"

<u>   t   </u>

UP-TILL-NOW, HEAR NONE INDEX-*lf*

- <u>   nodding   </u>
  FINISH APPLY OTHER #JOB ME,

  Notice that Lee responds affirmatively to Pat's question by nodding while providing more specific information. For further information about this use of nodding, see Unit 1.

- <u>   brow raise   </u>
  ME+ *me*-**SEND-TO**-*lf*

  The sign *me*-**SEND-TO**-*lf* is an example of a sign which can indicate the subject and object by its direction of movement. (See Unit 4 for further information about directional verbs). Notice that Lee does not specifically mention the place or company where s/he applied, but still gives a location to the left.

- **WAIT**"*long time*"

  This is another example of the *"long time"* movement. Remember that the Signer's perception is important in using these time-related movements. Thus, maybe
  Lee applied just three weeks ago but feels that three
  weeks is a long time (or maybe s/he applied three months
  ago!). No specific time is given, just that Lee feels it has
  been a long time.

- $\overline{\text{UP-TILL-NOW}}^{\,t}$

  Notice that this sign occurs with the non-manual behaviors used to indicate a *topic*. See Unit 1 for a description of
  these behaviors.

- **HEAR NONE   INDEX**-*lf*

  The sign **HEAR NONE** is another example of two signs
  made in such a way that they look like a single sign.
  Compare the illustration of this sign with the illustration
  of the sign **SEE**-*you* **NONE** to get an idea of some of the
  changes which occur with the signs **SEE**-*you,* **HEAR,** and
  NONE.
     The sign **INDEX**-*lf* refers to the company or place
  where Lee applied for a job. Lee points to the left because
  that is the location that was assigned to the company or
  place with the sign *me*-**SEND-TO**-*lf*.

I. Sample Drills

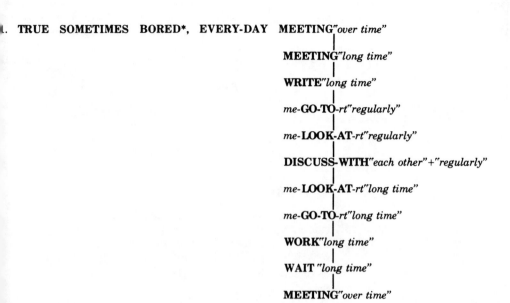

1. TRUE SOMETIMES BORED*, EVERY-DAY MEETING"*over time*"

MEETING"*long time*"

WRITE"*long time*"

me-GO-TO-*rt*"*regularly*"

me-LOOK-AT-*rt*"*regularly*"

DISCUSS-WITH"*each other*"+"*regularly*"

me-LOOK-AT-*rt*"*long time*"

me-GO-TO-*rt*"*long time*"

WORK"*long time*"

WAIT "*long time*"

MEETING"*over time*"

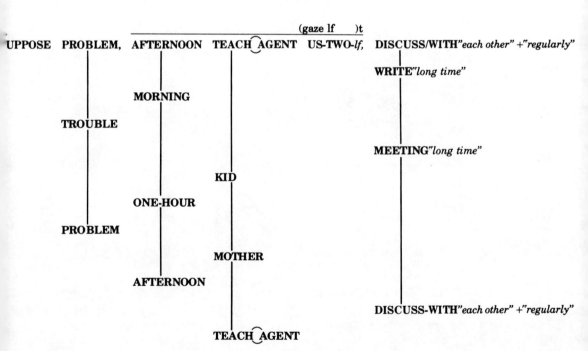

                         (gaze lf   )t

UPPOSE PROBLEM, AFTERNOON TEACH AGENT US-TWO-*lf*, DISCUSS/WITH"*each other*" +"*regularly*"

WRITE"*long time*"

MORNING

TROUBLE

MEETING"*long time*"

KID

ONE-HOUR

PROBLEM

MOTHER

AFTERNOON

DISCUSS-WITH"*each other*" +"*regularly*"

TEACH AGENT

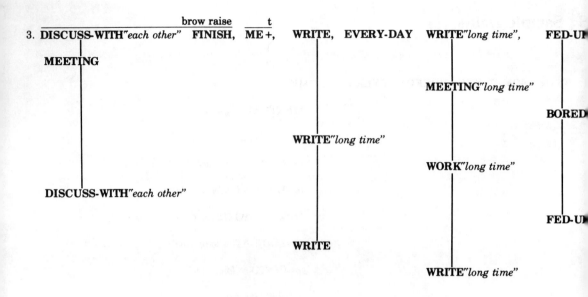

3. DISCUSS-WITH"*each other*" FINISH, ME+, WRITE, EVERY-DAY

I. Video Notes

If you have access to the videotape package designed to accompany these texts, you will notice the following:

- Notice that Pat provides constant feedback to Lee while he is explaining about his job. The feedback is both manual and non-manual and serves to reassure Lee that Pat understands and is following him.

   The non-manual feedback occurs in the form of head nodding and shaking at appropriate places and facial expressions that show surprise, interest, concern, and dismay. The manual feedback (which occurs while Lee is signing) can be seen in signs like **FINE, TRUE, OH-I-SEE,** and **AWFUL.**

- Notice that there is one instance where Pat repeats what Lee has signed (**HEAR͡NONE**). This is another common way of providing the Signer with feedback.

- Notice that Lee's third and fourth turns are actually one long turn. During this long turn, there are several instances where Pat provides manual and non-manual feedback. Lee responds positively to this feedback and continues signing until Pat asks the question about quitting the job.

- Notice the particular movements used with the verbs **DISCUSS-WITH, MEETING, WRITE,** and **WAIT**. The 'one shot' of Lee provides clear examples of the special movements called *"long time"*, *"regularly"*, and *"over time"*.

Unit 9

Distributional Aspect

A. Synopsis

Pat and Lee were, at one time, actively involved in demonstrating for the rights of Deaf people. They are having dinner at a restaurant and Pat asks if Lee remembers the 504 demonstration last year with the Deaf people, Blind people, and people in wheelchairs. Lee remembers and asks if Pat remembers the man who was on the platform talking away and the woman who passed out papers for everyone to sign and then collected the papers and gave them to the man. Pat asks if Lee remembers that some people there asked the man some questions and he was hesitant and unsure, so some people started insulting him. Lee remembers and says that s/he thought the police might come and arrest some of the people. Pat asks what Lee would do if the police arrested him/her. Lee says that s/he doesn't know—probably say nothing and let them take him/her away. Pat says that if that happened, Deaf people all over the U.S. would send letters of complaint, and the police wouldn't be able to say anything. Lee doesn't believe that with the people at the meeting—Deaf, Blind, and so on—the police would have arrested anyone. Pat agrees and reminds Lee that the T.V. cameras were recording everything and that they would show whatever happened. Lee remembers and says that the headlines in the paper the next morning would have caused them some embarrassment.

B. Cultural Information: Section 504 and the American Coalition of Citizens with Disabilities

The Rehabilitation Act of 1973 was a milestone for millions of disabled Americans. This Act contained one particular section—Section 504—which said that no program receiving federal funding could discriminate against a person solely on the basis of his or her disability. Prior to Section 504, disabled persons were often denied admission to the college of their choice, discriminated against in the job market, denied services by clinics, were often unable to take advantage of public housing and, in general, were unable to take advantage of thousands of federally-supported programs. Section 504 was designed to put an end to such discrimination and to make all such programs accessible to disabled persons.

Although the law was passed in 1973, no real action was taken to implement it until 1977 when the rules and regulations were signed. This signing would not have happened, however, without some pressure from disabled citizens. When the American Coalition of Citizens with Disabilities (ACCD) learned that the government was considering rewriting and substantially weakening the regulations, it called for nationwide demonstrations of protest. On April 5, 1977, thousands of disabled

150

Americans all over the nation staged protests and sit-ins. The regulations were signed on April 28, 1977.

The American Coalition of Citizens with Disabilities (ACCD) is a national association of more than 75 national, state, and local organizations of and for almost every category of disabled people. More than seven million of the nation's 36 million disabled citizens are represented by the organizations that belong to the ACCD. For more information about Section 504 and the ACCD, write: American Coalition of Citizens with Disabilities, 1200 15th Street N.W., Suite 201, Washington, D.C. 20005.

C. Dialogue

Pat

Pat₁:
$$\overline{\overset{co}{}}$$
"UMMM" **REMEMBER YOU ONE-YEAR-PAST**wg, **DEAF BLIND WHEELCHAIR,**

$$\overline{}\overset{q}{}\quad\overline{}\overset{q}{}$$
INDEX-_arc-rt_ **(2h)alt.COMPLAIN REBEL FIVE ZERO FOUR, REMEMBER**
YOU

Pat₂:
$$\overline{}\overset{q}{}$$
"THAT'S-RIGHT" +, **REMEMBER THAT-ONE MAN GIVE-LECTURE,**
INDEX-lf ⟶

$$\overline{}\overset{t}{}$$
INDEX-_arc-cntr_ **PEOPLE,** _"unspecified"people_-**ASK-TO**-_man,_

(body shift to lf   )
MAN "hesitant and unsure", **PEOPLE** _"unspecified"people_-**INSULT-TO**-_man_

Pat₃:
$$\overline{}\overset{wh\text{-}q}{}$$
"WELL" "PSHAW" "WELL", SUPPOSE POLICE _police_-**ARREST**-_you,_ **#DO-DO YOU**

Pat₄:
"WELL", SUPPOSE HAPPEN,

DEAF PEOPLE ALL-OVER U-S, _"unspecified"people_-**SEND-TO**-_cntr_ **(2h)alt.COMPLAIN,**

$$\overline{}\overset{t}{}$$
POLICE, "hesitant" **GULP**

Pat₅:
$$\overline{}\overset{nodding}{}\quad\overline{}\overset{q}{}$$
TRUE++, REMEMBER YOU #TV+ CAMERA-RECORD-_arc,_ **CAMERA-RECORD**-_arc_ ↔

Lee

Lee₁: **RIGHT YOU RIGHT YOU,**

                    (gaze up,rt   )
    REMEMBER MAN V-CL-*up,rt*'stand on platform' **GIVE-LECTURE**"*regularly*",

    _____t (gaze lf   )
    PAPER, WOMAN *woman-***GIVE-TO-***people*"*all*" **PEOPLE** "*all*"*people-***SIGN-NAME,**

    WOMAN COLLECT-*papers*"*all*"   **C-CL** } 'thick stack of papers'
                                       B↑-CL }

    *woman-***GIVE-***stack of papers-***TO-***man*

Lee₂: **RIGHT*, THAT-ONE* PERIOD-OF-TIME, ME FEEL +**

                                                                    neg
    POLICE FROM-*lf-***ASSEMBLE-TO-***cntr* *police-***ARREST-***people*"*unspecified*" ‾‾‾‾‾‾

           _____q   _____neg   _____neg
Lee₃: *police-***ARREST-***me,* **NOT-KNOW, SAY-NOTHING** *police-***TAKE-***me-***AWAY-***rt,* **NOT-KNOW**

                                                              t
Lee₄: **PEOPLE MEETING INDEX-***rt* **DEAF BLIND VARIOUS-THINGS,**

                                                      q   neg
    TRUE WORK POLICE *police-***ARREST-***people* "*unspecified*", **DISBELIEVE ME DISBELIEVE**wg

                                                             t
Lee₅: **RIGHT YOU, ONE-DAY-FUTURE MORNING NEWSPAPER,**

                                (gaze rt) (gaze lf   )
    L:-CL } 'newspaper headline' **INDEX-***rt* **(2h)BECOME-EMBARRASSED**
    B↑-CL }

D. Key Illustrations

Pat

(2h)alt.COMPLAIN

REBEL

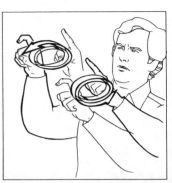

"unspecified"people-ASK-TO-*man*

"unspecified"people-INSULT-TO-*man*

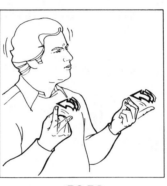

#DO-DO

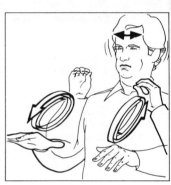

"unspecified"people-SEND-TO-*cntr*

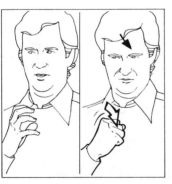

GULP

CAMERA-RECORD-*arc*

Lee

woman-GIVE-TO-*people"all"*

"all"people-SIGN-NAME

COLLECT-*papers"all"*

woman-GIVE-*stack of papers*-TO-*man*

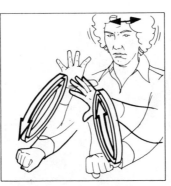

police-ARREST-*people"unspecified"*

SAY-NOTHING

TRUE⌣WORK

DISBELIEVE

L:↑-CL }
B↑-CL }   'newspaper headline'

E. Supplementary Illustrations

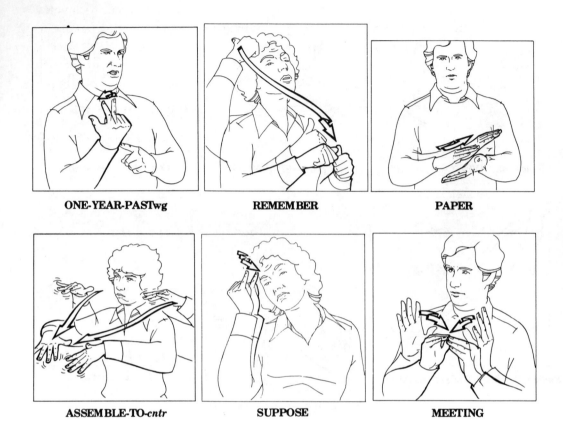

ONE-YEAR-PASTwg   REMEMBER   PAPER

ASSEMBLE-TO-*cntr*   SUPPOSE   MEETING

F. General Discussion: Distributional Aspect

The term *distributional aspect* refers to certain movements that occur with verbs to indicate how an action is "distributed". For example, does the action happen to everyone? Does it happen to each person separately, one after the other? Does it happen at different times to specific persons? Or, does it happen at different times to a lot of people? These are some of the things that can also be shown by adding certain movements to verbs.

One of these movements involves what we call a "sweep" of one or both of the hands in an arc. The Signer's eyes and head usually move from one side to the other in an arc, too, when this movement is added to a verb. This movement shows that the action happens to everyone (or everything); so we call this movement "*all*".

For example, suppose you are a Deaf teacher and you are going to give your class a test. The students are frantically doing some "last minute" studying, so you wait a few minutes and then ask them if they are ready. To describe the action of asking the students, you might use the sign illustrated below. This sign indicates that you asked 'them' or 'all the students'.

me-ASK-TO- *students"all"*

The students groan and say "OK", so you pass out (give) the test papers to 'them' or 'all the students'.

me-GIVE-TO-*students"all"*

Notice that this movement of the verb gives the idea of a single action. You might actually have given out the papers to each student one-by-one (which would be many, separate actions), but instead you choose to describe the action as one event. This is like saying, in English, 'I gave them the test papers' instead of 'I gave each of them a test paper'. This second way of describing the event (as many separate actions) would involve a different movement of the verb.

This *"all"* movement of the verb also shows the spatial location of the people or things involved in the action. In the two illustrations above, the signs refer to all of the students so the verb moves from one side to the other. But suppose there are two groups of students in the room. The students on the right side of the room are older and more advanced, so you, the teacher, give them less time to take the test and collect their test papers first. This action of collecting their papers could be described as:

me-COLLECT-*papers"all"-rt*

Here the 'arc' of the verb only includes the papers of the students located to the right. The meaning of the verb is still 'all of them', but only refers to a particular group.

Now let's look at another kind of movement that indicates how an action is "distributed". This movement is made with both hands alternating in a somewhat circular manner. The Signer usually does not look at any particular place while making a sign with this kind of movement, but his/her head usually 'bobs' with each alternating movement. Like the *"all"* movement (modulation), this movement does not focus on specific individuals. However, this movement does indicate that some or many individuals are involved in the event.

For example, suppose you are at a rally for "Energy Conservation" and you are passing out leaflets to various people as they walk by. Each time you give out a leaflet, that's one action, and the action is repeated over and over again. You are not focusing on giving the leaflet to specific individuals, but just anyone who will take one from you. Thus, this event (giving out the leaflet) involves many separate actions with non-specific individuals. The movement that describes this kind of distribution is called *"unspecified"* since it does not focus on specific individuals.

*me-**GIVE-TO**-people"unspecified"*

Similarly, suppose there are many speakers at the rally. After they finish their talks, the speakers line up on the platform so the audience can ask them questions. You are a staunch conservationist and have a variety of "burning questions" you want to ask various speakers. When you get your chance, you fire off your questions to the people you want to respond to them. What you did might be described with the sign illustrated below:

*me-**ASK-TO**-speakers"unspecified"*

Again, notice that with this *"unspecified"* movement (modulation), the meaning is more like 'fired away lots of questions at various people'. This movement does not focus on the specific individuals who were asked the questions. (If the Signer wanted to focus on specific individuals, s/he would use a different modulation.)

The two movements described in this section, *"all"* and *"unspecified"*, occur with directional verbs (see Unit 4)—where the movement of the verb also indicates the subject and/or the object. Thus, the sign *me-**COLLECT**-papers"all"-rt* moved from the Signer toward the group of older students located to the right and then moved in an arc across that location. Similarly, returning to the context of the rally, if one of the speakers spoke against energy conservation, s/he would probably receive lots of angry letters. This person might describe his/her experience with the sign illustrated below, meaning 'many unspecified individuals send letters to me'. (The facial expression and turned head shows how the Signer feels about receiving all those angry letters!)

*"unspecified"people-*SEND-TO-*me*

This sign moves toward the Signer (the object) and has the semi-circular, alternating movement which indicates that the action involves various "unspecified" individuals.

Once again, you can see how certain types of movements have specific meanings. Various movements can occur together with one sign (like a directional verb). Thus, a given sign in ASL can be very complex and communicate a great deal of information.

G. Text Analysis

            co

Pat₁: ―――

       "UMMM" **REMEMBER YOU ONE-YEAR-PAST**wg, **DEAF BLIND WHEELCHAIR,**

                                                               q ―――――――― q

INDEX-*arc-rt* **(2h)alt.COMPLAIN REBEL FIVE ZERO FOUR, REMEMBER**

                                                                               YOU

- **ONE-YEAR-PAST**wg

  This is an example of a time sign which is made in relation to the time line. The sign moves toward the area
  behind the Signer's body—'toward the past'. Notice in the
  illustration how the index finger flicks or wiggles toward
  the 'past'. A variation of this sign is illustrated below. In
  this variation the whole hand moves toward the 'past'.

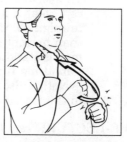

  ONE-YEAR-PAST

- **INDEX-***arc-rt*

  This is an example of a plural pronoun. Here the pronoun
  refers to the **DEAF BLIND WHEELCHAIR** people and
  also gives them a specific location (to the Signer's right).

- **FIVE ZERO FOUR**

  It is interesting that when referring to this section of the
  law, these numbers are not signed **FIVE HUNDRED
  FOUR**. Rather each number is signed separately. In
  spoken English, this section of the law is also referred to
  as "five oh four", not "five hundred and four".

- **REMEMBER**   q

                      YOU

  Notice that the Signer began and ended the turn with
  these signs. This repetition is similar to what sometimes
  occurs in English—"Remember that party last month?
  Huh?" or "You know that white sailboat? You know the
  one I mean?"

Lee₁: **RIGHT YOU RIGHT YOU,**

                               (gaze up,rt   )
REMEMBER   MAN   V-CL-*up,rt*'stand on platform'   **GIVE-LECTURE**"*regularly*",

           _____t_ (gaze lf   )
PAPER,   WOMAN   *woman*-**GIVE-TO**-*people*"*all*"   **PEOPLE**   "*all*"*people*-**SIGN-NAME,**

WOMAN   COLLECT-*papers*"*all*"   C-CL ⎫
                                    B↑-CL⎭ 'thick stack of papers'

woman-**GIVE**-*stack of papers*-**TO**-*man*

-   (gaze up,rt   )
  V-CL-*up,rt*'*stand on platform*'

  This is an example of a classifier (Unit 5) which is used to represent a man standing. (Compare this classifier with the sign **STAND**). Because the classifier is located higher than normal to the Signer's right, it is apparent that the man is standing above the crowd of people, presumably on something like a stage or platform.

  Notice also that the Signer looks up and to the right—to the location where the classifier is placed.

- **GIVE-LECTURE**"*regularly*"

  Notice that this sign uses the movement described in Unit 8 to indicate that the action ('giving a talk or lecture') occurred a lot or kept going on and on.

- *woman*-**GIVE-TO**-*people*"*all*"

  This is an example of a verb with the "*all*" movement that is described above. Notice that the meaning is 'the woman gave out the papers to all the people in the group'. The focus here is on the fact that the woman gave out papers to the *group,* not to specific individuals within the group.

- "*all*"*people*-**SIGN-NAME**

  This is another example of a verb with the sweeping, arc movement that we write as "*all*". Notice that the Signer uses the same "*all*" movement for this sign as was used for the sign *woman*-**GIVE-TO**-*people*"*all*". Thus, the Signer maintains a consistent focus while describing this event.

- **COLLECT-***papers*"*all*"

  Here again the Signer describes the event (collecting the papers) as a single action, rather than as many separate actions (collecting each of the papers).

  Notice also that the Signer has maintained a consistent perspective in describing the series of events by using the same modulation ("*all*") during this turn.

- C-CL ⎱
  B↑-CL ⎰ 'thick stack of papers'   *woman-GIVE-stack of papers-TO-man*

    C-CL
The classifiers *B↑-CL* represent the stack of papers which
the woman collected from the group. The C-CL classifier
is maintained in the next sign.

    When a classifier is used in the sign ____-GIVE-TO-
____, the sign not only indicates who gave and who re-
ceived, but it also indicates *what* was given. Thus, the
sign here is glossed as ____-GIVE-____-TO-____. For
example, a Signer could use the handshape on the left to
convey the meaning 'someone gives a credit card to someone else', or the handshape on the right to convey the
meaning 'someone gives a cup to someone else'.

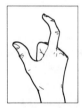

q

Pat₂: "THAT'S-RIGHT" +, <u>REMEMBER THAT-ONE MAN GIVE-LECTURE,</u>
                    INDEX-lf ⎯⎯⎯⎯⎯⎯⎯⎯→

<u>   t</u>
INDEX-*arc-cntr* **PEOPLE**, *"unspecified"people-***ASK-TO**-*man,*

        (body shift to lf   )
MAN "hesitant and unsure", **PEOPLE** *"unspecified"people-***INSULT-TO**-*man*

- *"unspecified"people-ASK-TO-man*

    This is an example of a verb in which the subject is *"un-
specified"*. Notice in the illustration of this sign that the
movement of the verb is toward the location of the
man—toward the upper right. Compare this illustration
with the one below in which the *"unspecified"* movement
is used to describe the object of the verb (various people).

me-ASK-TO-*people"unspecified"*

(body shift to lf   )
- **MAN**   "hesitant and unsure"

> Notice that the Signer mimes the reactions of the man by "role playing" or "becoming" the man. Notice also that the Signer's body shifts to the left (to the location previously assigned to the man) while assuming the character of the man.

- *"unspecified"people*-**INSULT-TO**-*man*

> This is also an example of a verb with the *"unspecified"* movement. Notice that the focus is on the fact that various people within the group performed the action and that it was directed toward a single person.

Lee$_2$:   **RIGHT***, **THAT-ONE*** **PERIOD-OF-TIME**, **ME** **FEEL**+

<u>neg</u>

POLICE **FROM**-*lf*-**ASSEMBLE-TO**-*cntr*   *police*-**ARREST**-*people"unspecified"*

- **FROM**-*lf*-**ASSEMBLE-TO**-*cntr*

> This is an example of a plural classifier (**5↓wg-CL**) which has become a "conventional" (widely used and accepted) sign. This classifier is often used to show a large number of people or animals that are in motion. Used as a verb, this classifier can indicate both movement from a particular location and movement toward another location (Unit 6).

- *police*-**ARREST**-*people"unspecified"*

> Once again notice the use of the *"unspecified"* movement. This time, however, it refers to the object of the verb, not the subject.

- <u>neg</u>

> Notice that after explaining what s/he thought might happen, the Signer responds to his/her own comments with the negative non-manual behaviors (Unit 1) to show that it really didn't happen or that the Signer's initial feeling was wrong.

Pat₃: "WELL" "PSHAW" "WELL",   SUPPOSE   POLICE   *police*-**ARREST**-*you*,   **#DO-DO YOU**

- **SUPPOSE POLICE** *police*-**ARREST**-*you*

    This is an example of a *condition* in a conditional sentence. Generally the condition (If . . .) is stated first, followed by the consequence or result (. . . then . . .). Conditionals in ASL can be introduced by using the sign **SUPPOSE** or the loan signs **#IF** or **#IFwg**, or may occur without these signs. Conditionals always occur with specific nonmanual behaviors (which include a brow raise).

-           wh-q
  #DO-DO YOU

    Notice that this question concerns the 'consequence' of the conditional discussed above. Notice also that the nonmanual behaviors used for 'wh-word' questions occur throughout the question. See Unit 1 for a description of these behaviors.

         q   neg   neg

Lee₃: *police*-**ARREST**-*me,*   **NOT-KNOW**,   **SAY-NOTHING**   *police*-**TAKE**-*me*-**AWAY**-*rt,*   **NOT-KNOW**

-                q
  police-**ARREST**-*me*

    Notice that the sign ____-**ARREST**-____ is used by both Pat and Lee. In both cases, the direction of movement makes it clear that 'police' is the subject and 'Lee' is the object. For further information about directional verbs like ____-**ARREST**-____ , see Unit 4.

- **SAY-NOTHING**

    This sign is very similar to another sign which can be glossed as **I-DIDN'T-MEAN-THAT.** Compare the illustrations of these two signs below. Notice that in the sign **SAY-NOTHING**, the head moves toward the index finger while in the other sign, the index finger moves toward the head. Notice also the difference in facial behaviors.

SAY-NOTHING   **I-DIDN'T-MEAN-THAT**

- *police*-**TAKE**-*me*-**AWAY**-*rt*

    This is an example of a directional verb (Unit 4) which can indicate not only the subject ('police') and the object ('me'), but also a specific direction or location to which the object is taken.

Pat₄: "WELL", SUPPOSE HAPPEN,

DEAF PEOPLE ALL-OVER U-S, *"unspecified"people-***SEND-TO**-*cntr*   (2h)alt.**COMPLAIN,**

_____t
POLICE, "hesitant" **GULP**

- **SUPPOSE HAPPEN**

    This is another example of a *condition* in a conditional sentence. The action of the 'deaf people all over the U.S.' is the consequence or result.

- *"unspecified"people-***SEND-TO**-*cntr*

    Notice that the subject of this verb is *"unspecified"* and indicates that various Deaf people would send letters of complaint to the police.

- **POLICE** "hesitant"

    This is another example of the use of role playing. In this case, the Signer 'acts out' the response of the police to the letters of complaint.

- **GULP**

    This sign is not easily translatable into English. The meaning it conveys is one of being caught in an embarrassing situation or being proven wrong and then not having anything to say or not being able to say anything.

                                                                    t
Lee₄: PEOPLE MEETING INDEX-*rt* DEAF BLIND VARIOUS-THINGS,

_____q _____neg
TRUE⌣WORK POLICE *police-***ARREST-***people "unspecified",* DISBELIEVE ME DISBELIEVEwg

- **TRUE⌣WORK**

    This is another example of two signs which frequently occur together. As with other signs like this, there are certain changes which occur when these two signs are used in combination with each other. The meaning which this sign conveys is something like 'seriously', 'no fooling around', or 'really and truly'.

- _____neg
    DISBELIEVE ME DISBELIEVEwg

    Notice that the Signer responds negatively or skeptically to his/her own question ('Would the police really have arrested some of the people?').

$$\text{Pat}_5:\quad \overset{\text{nodding}}{\underset{}{\text{TRUE}++,}}\ \overline{\text{REMEMBER}\quad \text{YOU}\quad \#\text{TV}+\quad \text{CAMERA-RECORD-}arc,}{}^{\text{q}}\quad \text{CAMERA-RECORD-}arc \leftrightarrow$$

- nodding
  TRUE++

  > Here Pat agrees with Lee's feeling that the police would
  > not arrest anyone. Notice the head nodding and repetition
  > of the sign **TRUE**.

- **#TV+**

  > This is another example of a fingerspelled loan sign in
  > ASL.

- **CAMERA-RECORD-***arc*,   **CAMERA-RECORD-***arc*↔

  > If you examine the illustration, you will notice a similar-
  > ity between the *arc* movement and the movement used to
  > convey the meaning *"all"*. Here the Signer is remember-
  > ing how the t.v. camera was recording everything that
  > was happening.
  >
  > Remember that the double-headed arrow (↔) indicates
  > a back and forth movement.

$$\text{Lee}_5:\quad \textbf{RIGHT}\quad \textbf{YOU,}\quad \overline{\textbf{ONE-DAY-FUTURE MORNING}\quad \textbf{NEWSPAPER,}}{}^{\text{t}}$$

$$\left.\begin{array}{l}\text{L:-CL}\\ B\uparrow\text{-CL}\end{array}\right\}\ \text{'newspaper headline'}\quad \overset{(\text{gaze rt })}{\textbf{INDEX-}rt}\quad \overset{(\text{gaze lf}\qquad\qquad)}{\textbf{(2h)BECOME-EMBARRASSED}}$$

- $\overline{\textbf{ONE-DAY-FUTURE MORNING}}{}^{\text{t}}$

  > This is another example of two signs which frequently
  > occur together. Again, there are certain changes that take
  > place when these two signs (**ONE-DAY-FUTURE** and
  > **MORNING**) are used in combination. When they do occur
  > in combination, the meaning is 'the next morning', 'the
  > morning after', or 'tomorrow morning'.

H. Sample Drills

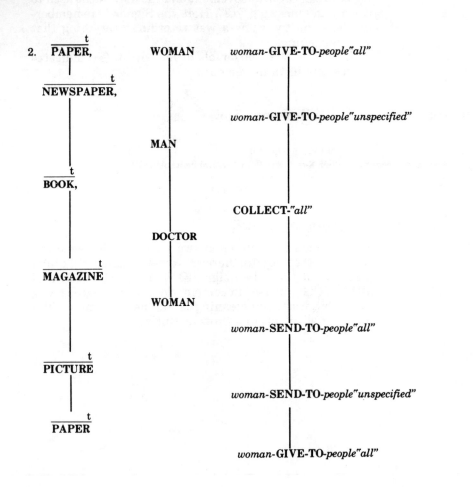

1. SUPPOSE POLICE *police-*ARREST*-you,*   wh-q
                                                #DO-DO YOU

        *police-*ARREST*-people"unspecified"*

        *police-*INSULT-TO*-people"unspecified"*

        *police-*GIVE-TO*-people"unspecified"*

        *police-*SEND-TO*-people"unspecified"*

        *police-*SHOOT-AT*-people"unspecified"*

        *police-*THROW-AT*-people"unspecified"*

        *police-*ARREST*-you*

2.   t
    PAPER,   WOMAN   *woman-*GIVE-TO*-people"all"*

           t
    NEWSPAPER,
                                   *woman-*GIVE-TO*-people"unspecified"*

                      MAN

     t
    BOOK,   COLLECT*-"all"*

                      DOCTOR

         t
    MAGAZINE
                      WOMAN
                                   *woman-*SEND-TO*-people"all"*

        t
    PICTURE
                                   *woman-*SEND-TO*-people"unspecified"*

      t
    PAPER
                                   *woman-*GIVE-TO*-people"all"*

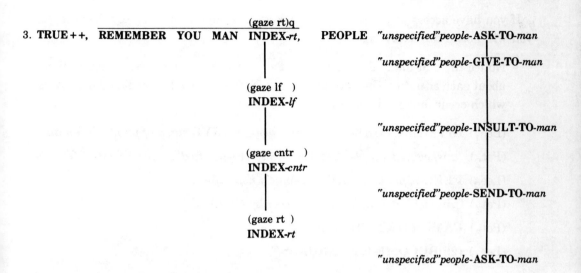

3. TRUE++, REMEMBER YOU MAN INDEX-*rt*, PEOPLE ...

I. Video Notes

If you have access to the videotape package designed to accompany these texts, you will notice the following:

- Notice the non-manual behaviors of Pat and Lee which express their feelings about each situation they are discussing. Notice especially the facial behaviors which occur during the signs:

    (Lee$_1$) **GIVE-LECTURE-***"regularly"*, *woman*-**GIVE**-*stack of papers*-**TO**-*man*

    (Pat$_2$) *"unspecified"people*-**ASK-TO**-*man,* *"unspecified"people*-**INSULT-TO**-*man*

    (Lee$_2$) **FEEL +,** *police*-**ARREST**-*people"unspecified"*

    (Pat$_4$) *"unspecified"people*-**SEND-TO**-*cntr,* **GULP**

    (Pat$_5$) **CAMERA-RECORD**-*arc*

    (Lee$_5$) **(2h)BECOME-EMBARRASSED**

- Notice the special verb movements used to indicate *"all"* and *"unspecified"*. The 'one shot' segments of Pat and Lee provide excellent views of these movements.

- Notice how the signs **TRUE⌒WORK** and **ONE-DAY-FUTURE⌒MORNING** are made. Pay particular attention to the changes which happen because these signs occur in a combination.

- Notice the feedback which Pat and Lee give each other—head nods and facial behaviors which reinforce the descriptions and statements of each Signer.

Video Package Notes:

If you have access to the videotape package designed to accompany these texts, you will see the following stories and narrative descriptions which appear after dialogues 1–9.

Friends—Pat Graybill
In this first short narrative, notice that the entire story is told using signs with the extended index finger.

The Tree—Gilbert C. Eastman
This touching story describes the life of a tree. Notice how the Signer's facial expression indicates the range of feelings and moods of the tree as well as how the appearance of the tree changes.

The Highdiver—M. J. Bienvenu
This story tells of the triumph of a courageous highdiver and is told almost exclusively with classifier handshapes. Notice how they are used in setting the scene and in describing the action.

The Highdiver—Gilbert C. Eastman
This story is a variation of the first highdiver story. Notice the similarities and differences in setting the scene and describing the action.

Fourth of July—Pat Graybill
This narrative uses a variety of classifier handshapes to show the location and movement of the fireworks.

How Many Indians?—Ella Lentz
This narrative is a "play on handshapes". Notice that the Signer uses the handshapes which correspond to the numbers 1–15 in telling the story.

Fun With Fives—M. J. Bienvenu
This narrative is also a "play on handshapes". Notice that the entire story is told with signs that have the same handshape as the number 5.

Don't Count Your Chickens Before They're Hatched—Larry Berke
In this narrative, notice how the school is located to the Signer's left and the home is located to the Signer's right. Body shifts and changes in facial expression are used to show what the teacher says and what the mother says.

Differences—Nathie Couthen
This true story illustrates the dialogue and actions of two young girls. Notice how the Signer changes body position and facial expression as she "becomes" each character.

The Fearful Fisherman—Larry Berke
This amusing story uses a clever combination of signs and mimed actions to show a young boy's fearful experience while fishing.

INDEX OF ILLUSTRATIONS

The following is a list of all of the sign illustrations in this text. The illustrations for each unit are listed alphabetically according to their glosses. In cases where the illustration appears in more than one unit, those units are listed on the right.

Unit 1
Sentence Types

Unit 2
Time

173

HOME . . . 4

MEETING . . . 8, 9

MIDNIGHT

MORNING

NOON

NOT-YET . . . 1, 5, 7

"THAT'S-RIGHT"

THREE-MONTH

(2h)THRILL

TWO-WEEK-FUTURE (Variant A)

TWO-WEEK-FUTURE (Variant B)

TWO-WEEK-PAST

TWO-YEAR-FUTURE

"UMMM" . . . 1, 3, 4, 8

(2h)WHAT'S-UP . . . 6, 8

Unit 3
Pronominalization

CHAT

DEAF . . . 2

DEAF (formal) . . . 2

GO-*rt*

GROUP (relatively large)

GROUP (relatively small)

HIM/HER (honorific)

KNOW

KNOW-THAT . . . 1

ME (honorific)

MYSELF (variant a)

MYSELF (variant b)

OH-I-SEE . . . 7

ONE-YEAR-PAST . . . 2, 9

ONLY-ONE-*me*

ONLY-ONE-*you*

OURSELVES

PAST NIGHT . . . 6

SEVERAL

SPECIALTY-FIELD

THEREABOUTS-*rt* . . . 7

THINK SAME

TWO-DAY-PAST

"UMMM" . . . 1, 2, 4, 8

US-TWO-*rt*

VARIOUS-THINGS . . . 1

WE (others present)

WE (others not present)

YOURSELVES-AND-MYSELF

Unit 4
Subjects and Objects

me-ASK-TO-*lf* . . . 1

BROTHER

me-FLATTER-*you*

s/he-FLATTER-*me*

INFLUENCE-*mother*

INVESTIGATE-*mother*++

KNOW-NOTHING

MEDICINE

Unit 5
Classifiers

Unit 6
Locatives

BORROW-FROM-*you*

FROM-*atlanta*-FLY-TO-*here* . . . 4

FROM-*here*-FLY-TO-*atlanta* . . . 4

FROM-*here*-FLY-TO-*rt*

rt-GIVE-TO-*me* . . . 4

HAVE-OPERATION-ON-*head*

HAVE-OPERATION-ON-*heart*

HAVE-OPERATION-ON-*shoulder*

HOWwg . . . 4, 5

NOT͜ HERE

NOTICE-TO-*rt*

NOT-KNOW

NOT-POSSIBLE

PAST͜ NIGHT . . . 3

REMEMBER . . . 9

ROOMMATE

SEEM + . . . 4

SOMEONE/SOMETHING . . . 8

SNATCHED-UP-*trophy*

STEAL

THAT-ONE

TOURNAMENT

TROPHY

(2h)"WHAT" . . . 1, 5, 8

(2h)WHAT'S-UP . . . 2, 8

A-CL @*rt*'trophy on table'
C-CL @*rt*'cup behind trophy'

C-CL-*rt* ⎱ 'cup on table is
B⥮CL-*rt* ⎰ turned on its side'

3→CL'car stopped'
3→CL'car from left smash into left rear' . . . 5

Unit 7
Pluralization

AGE-THREE-*lf*

AGE-SEVEN-*rt*

COMMUTE-BETWEEN-*here*-AND-*rt*

CURIOUS

FEW

GO-TO-*rt* . . . 2

HEARING . . . 4

HOW-MANY

HUSBAND

KID

MEET + + + *arc*

(2h)NOTHING*

SKILL*

"SO-SO"

STATE-SCHOOL . . . 1, 8

STRANGE

TEACH͜ AGENT

THEREABOUTS . . . 3

THOSE-THREE-*rt*

US-THREE

YOU-THREE

1→CL"*in a row*" (pencils)

(2h)alt.1→CL'pencils scattered'

(2h)A-CL"*in a row*" (trophies)

Unit 8
Temporal Aspect

Unit 9
Distributional Aspect

ASSEMBLE-TO-*cntr*

CAMERA-RECORD-*arc*

COLLECT-*papers"all"*

me-COLLECT-*papers"all"-rt*

(2h)alt.COMPLAIN

DISBELIEVE

#DO-DO . . . 1

me-GIVE-TO-*people"unspecified"* . . . 4, 6

me-GIVE-TO-*students"all"* . . . 4, 6

woman-GIVE-TO-*people"all"* . . . 4, 6

woman-GIVE-*stack of papers*-TO-*man*

ONE-YEAR-PASTwg . . . 2, 3

PAPER

REBEL

REMEMBER . . . 6

SAY-NOTHING

"unspecified"people-SEND-TO-*cntr*

"unspecified"people-SEND-TO-*me*

"all"people-SIGN-NAME

SUPPOSE . . . 8

TRUE WORK

L:-CL }
B↑-CL } 'newspaper headline'